HOW TO DO
STANDARD ENGLISH
ACCENTS

HOW TO DO

Standard English
ACCENTS

Edda Sharpe &

Jan Haydn Rowles

methuen | drama
LONDON • NEW YORK • OXFORD • NEW DELHI • SYDNEY

METHUEN DRAMA
Bloomsbury Publishing Plc
50 Bedford Square, London, WC1B 3DP, UK
1385 Broadway, New York, NY 10018, USA
29 Earlsfort Terrace, Dublin 2, Ireland

BLOOMSBURY, METHUEN DRAMA and the Methuen Drama logo are
trademarks of Bloomsbury Publishing Plc

First published in Great Britain by Oberon Books 2012
Reprinted with revisions in 2015, 2017, 2020
This edition published by Methuen Drama 2021

A catalogue record for this book is available from the British Library.

ISBN: PB: 978-1-3502-6770-1

Printed and bound in Great Britain

To find out more about our authors and books visit www.bloomsbury.com
and sign up for our newsletters.

WHAT'S IN THIS BOOK

WITH THANKS TO

Jeannette Nelson, Head of Voice, National Theatre, Lyn Darnley, Head of Voice, Royal Shakespeare Company, and all our fellow Accent Coaches who have supported us over the years. Our editors Andrew Walby and James Illman. James Hogan for his continued support in the *How To Do Accents* Series and all those at Oberon Books.

Jack Adams, Ben Allen, Arsher Ali, Nicola Collett, Deborah Cordery, Lucy Frederick, John Gillet, Edward Hicks, Wilbur Heynes and the Heynes family, Julie Legrand, Ashley McGuire, Octavia MacKenzie, Laura Rogers, Richard Ryder, Bethany Sharpe, Sarah Simmonds, Genievie Steele, Michelle Terry, Rachel Williams, David Willis, Rufus Gerrard Wright.

Special thanks to Steve Cooper (recording editor) and Terry O'Brien (vocal artist) both of whom gave their indisputable talents and unyielding generosity to this project.

INTRODUCTION

> RP, The Queen's English, Sloane, Estuary, Oxford English, BBC English, Heightened, Advanced Marked RP, or just plain 'Posh'? What exactly is a Standard English Accent?

In every drama school, in every English-speaking country, students from all over the world have to learn some form of Standard English Accent, and, what's more, voice and drama tutors have to teach it. But what exactly is it? How many varieties are there? And which one should they use when?

You will notice that we have called this book, *How To Do Standard English Accent**S***, and there is the clue.

In this book we aim to clarify the differences between a Standard English Accent which is considered ***neutral*** in terms of race, age, gender, occupation or social background, and ***Period***, or ***Class***-based accents, with their many varieties and styles. After all Hugh Grant may well sound 'posh' but it just wouldn't be right for Hamlet. Or if it were, it would be a contemporary Hamlet that went to an English Public School. And there's the rub.

A variety of Standard English Accent which came to prominence in the 1920s was called Received Pronunciation, or RP for short, the word 'received' being an old-fashioned word meaning 'accepted'. Accents are usually named after the area they come from, but RP didn't come from a *place*, so much as from a type of *person*. The original narrow definition of RP included only persons who had been educated at one of what in Britain are called 'public schools' (actually very expensive private schools) such as Eton, Harrow, Winchester and Rugby, and was based on the upper and upper-middle-class speech patterns of Middle and South Eastern English.

It was this narrow accent that was adopted by educators and used as a 'standard' to be taught and learned for public speaking, and thus for stage and broadcasting purposes. This was, to a certain extent, an accident of history. Had history taken a couple of different turns, a Hampshire or Yorkshire accent might have been the accent chosen as a 'standard'.

But the perception of what is considered 'standard' has, of course, changed over the course of time. The voices we associate with early BBC broadcasts, for instance, now sound extremely old-fashioned to most of us, and old 'RP' has strong resonances of authority, social status and economic power. Varieties of this old accent are now confined to a very small section of society, the older upper and upper middle classes, older actors and broadcasters.

The acting industry still demands a Neutral Standard English Accent which can unify everyone *without* placing them in terms of age, class or region and the accent we would consider 'standard' today is the one we hear being used by actors such as David Tennant, Janet McTeer or Kenneth Branagh.

In Part One of this book we describe this **NEW STANDARD ENGLISH ACCENT (NSEA).**

Hear it: Track 1 'Arthur the Rat' and *Track 2* 'Free Speech'.

Although clearly a southern English accent, it lacks strong local accent features, and is a useful tool that has the *convention* of being non gender, race, age, class or region specific. It is English, as opposed to Scottish, Welsh or Northern Irish, all of which have their own neutral standard accents. We finish Part One with a nod to the **Old Stage Standard** which really illustrates how different the sound used to be!

In Part Two of the book we describe some upper-class varieties of Standard English Accent. The first is **Traditional RP**, a catch-all accent that is quite distinct from a New Standard English Accent. We then venture into the accents of the **Imperial Lords and Ladies**, the **Military, Matrons and Landed Gentry**, the **Debs, Dandies and Bright Young Things**, the **Wartime Wendies and BBC Berties**, the **Sloane Rangers**, and finally we give a nod to the **New Wave**.

Get into the scene

Accents don't exist in a vacuum: they are made by living, breathing communities, subject to the vagaries of history, politics, peer pressure, climate, culture, economics and more. Putting any accent into its **historical, geographical** and **cultural** context is an important step towards owning it and making it real.

Historically the concept of a Standard English accent could be said to have begun when the term 'Received Pronunciation' was coined in 1869 by the linguist, A.J. Ellis.

Before 1870 many of the most eminent Victorians retained their regional accents throughout their lives. William Wordsworth had a Cumberland accent, Sir Robert Peel's was Midlands, and, in spite of being educated at Eton and Oxford, William Gladstone had a strong Lancashire accent. Then came the Education Act of 1870, pioneered through Parliament by W.E. Forster.

> *The Education Act of 1870 not only established the English public school*
> *as the melting pot of upper and middle-class speech and society, but also*
> *started a boom in English prep schools. Now the children of country squires,*

> *city nobility, army officers, imperial civil servants, small-town lawyers,*
> *doctors, clergymen, and suburban dentists could be brought together from*
> *the ages of 8 to 18, drawn from many parts of the country, and educated in*
> *one confined space, with one standard accent, often isolated market towns*
> *like Uppingham, Sherborne, Tonbridge and Worksop.*

McCrum et al, The Story of English, 1992.

This 'one standard accent' soon came to be associated with 'The Establishment', and something to aspire to and emulate, particularly within the middle classes in London.

> *It is the business of educated people to speak so that no one may be able to*
> *tell in what county their childhood was passed.*

A. Burrell, Recitation: A Handbook for Teachers
in Public Elementary School, 1891.

The term RP became a more widely used term after the phonetician, Daniel Jones, adopted it for the second edition of his *English Pronouncing Dictionary* (1924). This form of standard accent probably received its greatest public endorsement when Lord Reith, the first General Manager of the BBC (himself a Scot!), adopted it in 1922 as a broadcasting standard – hence the origins of the term **BBC English**. Reith believed Standard English, spoken with an RP accent would be the most widely understood variety of English, both here in the UK and overseas. He also believed that choosing a regional accent might run the risk of alienating some listeners(!). But since RP was the preserve of the aristocracy and expensive public schools, it still represented only a very small social minority.

The period immediately after the Second World War was a boom time for RP as educational and social advancement suddenly became a possibility for many more people. Those who were able to take advantage of these opportunities – be it in terms of education or career – often felt under considerable pressure to conform linguistically and thus adopt the accent of the Establishment, or at least modify their speech towards RP norms, and so this Standard English accent grew and spread.

Like any other accent, RP has also changed over the course of time. The old RP of the BBC now sounds extremely old-fashioned. In recent years virtually every accent of English has become represented in all walks of life to which people aspire – sport, the arts, the media, business, even the former strongholds of RP, such as the City, Civil Service and academia. As a result, fewer younger speakers with regional accents consider it necessary to adapt their speech. Indeed many young people from private and public schools often go to great lengths to disguise their upper and upper-middle-class accent by incorporating regional features into their speech, leading to new varieties such as the New Wave, explored on pages 201–210 of this book.

Geographically, the Standard English Accent is a little tricky to pin down. The contemporary standard sound has most in common with accents of the south east, although the historical roots of RP spread a little further than this;

> *RP is often believed to be based on southern accents, but in fact it has most in common with the dialects of the south-east Midlands: **Northamptonshire, Bedfordshire** and **Huntingdonshire**. Migration to **London** in the 14th and 15th centuries was mostly from the counties directly north of London rather than those directly south. There are differences both within and among the three counties mentioned, but a conglomeration emerged in London, and also mixed with some elements of **Essex** and **Middlesex** speech.*

> *Wikipedia, 2011.*

Not only this, but its origins have more to do with social class than with geography, so that two upper-class families living as far apart as Yorkshire and Kent can sound more alike than two working-class families from neighbouring counties!

Under the heading of 'geography' it may also be useful to consider environmental influences on the sound, such as the access to beautiful open spaces and elegant artefacts, that come from living in large, well-furnished homes and landscaped gardens, or the grand buildings and expansive playing fields of the schools.

Culturally, the values and beliefs that expanded the use of a standard accent included promotion of health and vitality through plenty of fresh air, and exercise of body and mind. Boys were encouraged in sports and the importance of leadership; girls were trained in the appreciation of art, music, dance and sewing, and all were imbued with tradition, discipline and religion. Reith's decision to use a standard accent for the BBC reflected the cultural climate of the time: 'You cannot raise social standards without raising speech standards,' observed one member of the 1926 'Advisory Committee on Spoken English'.

And although having a standard accent may no longer be considered a *social* necessity, having access to an accent that is free from indicators of gender, race, age, class or region, is still considered to be an invaluable skill for an actor.

HOW TO USE THIS BOOK

You can use the first half of this book as a complete course in How To Do A New Standard English Accent, or, if you are looking for a specific character type you may want to dive straight in to the upper-class varieties in the second half. Each variety is described in full as a stand-alone description so you can head straight for the one you need.

Whichever you choose, you will find the architecture of each accent broken into five areas: the **Foundations**, the **Groove**, the **Two Planets**, the **Bite** and the **Shapes**. These can be studied in any order.

To get the most out of the book we recommend you use your powers of: sensing, practising and processing.

Sensing

Being good at any accent is about so much more than 'having a good ear'. It is about using *all* your available senses to learn new skills, just as you did as a small child. For this reason we encourage you throughout the book to **see**, **feel** and **hear** the new accent.

Through the book you will see these 4 icons:

 This icon prompts you to focus in a visual way, either by looking at an illustration, using your mind's eye, or looking in a mirror.

 This icon prompts you to focus on physical processes and feelings.

 This icon prompts you to focus in an aural way by listening to a track on the downloadable MP3s. See page 234 for instructions on how to download the tracks that accompany this book.

 This icon also prompts you to focus in an aural way by listening to yourself.

Creating a Funnel

When learning new sounds it helps to have a way of listening to yourself that is instant and gives you an accurate 'outside ear' on the sounds you are making.

You can do this by 'funnelling' the sound from your mouth straight back to your ear.

Put one hand about five centimetres (two inches) away from your mouth, cup it onto the bottom of the other hand which then in turn cups behind the ear, creating a funnel from one to the other.

You will know you've got the position right when you hear your voice loud and clear, even when you are speaking quietly. This is invaluable when you are working in a group, or when you need to practise quietly!

Practising

When you were a child you dedicated hours to hearing the sounds and/or seeing the shapes of the faces around you, playing with the shape of your mouth, until the sounds and shapes *you* were making matched the sounds and shapes you were *hearing* and/or *seeing*. Then you practised those shapes and movements over and over again until they became locked into your muscle memory. That's what children do. That's what you did and how you learned to speak. That's why you have an accent, even if you think you haven't!

Remember, learning how to do a New Standard English Accent is just like anything else you've successfully learnt: riding a bike, speaking a language, or even navigating a new mobile phone. Some things seem to come easily; others seem to take longer to get into the muscle memory. Separate out the different elements, identify what you know, recognise what you don't know and then learn, relearn and above all *practise*. During this process your awareness is very high and the focus and juggling can seem complicated. Don't panic – keep calm – this just means there is more learning taking place! Soon the elements come together and the process seems natural and effortless.

Processing

To help you teach your left brain (where logic and structure live) to store the discoveries you are making, the Haydn/Sharpe system provides you with two tools.

● **Checklists**

   Each chapter has a summary of the main element it describes. When put together, these summaries will provide a quick checklist and overview of the elements of a New Standard English Accent.

● **You and the New**

   One thing that can really help you to do a new accent is an understanding of your *own* and how the new one differs from it.

If you already have our book *How To Do Accents*, you will be familiar with the **You and the New** chart. On our website www.howtodoaccents.com we have filled in the NEW section of a **You and the New** chart as for a New Standard English Accent. You may wish to fill in the YOU section. Once filled in, this will provide you with an instant comparison between your own and Neutral Standard English Accent, showing you where the most significant changes are.

Learning an accent is all about layering. Take it a piece at a time, practise all the pieces and then put them all together. And, above all, be prepared to make mistakes and sound silly: this is just you and your brain learning!

PART ONE

NEW STANDARD
ENGLISH ACCENT

15

1

THE FOUNDATIONS

IN THIS CHAPTER...

You will learn how to build the **Foundations** of a New Standard English Accent.

Having solid Foundations will hold the whole structure of the accent in place.

To establish solid New Standard English Foundations, you will need these three elements:

- **The Setting** – The setting of the muscles of the face and mouth.
- **The Zone** – Where the voice is focused.
- **The Tone** – The resonant quality of the voice.

With these in place, and because the voice is not a static building, you will need one more element...

- **The Direction** – The direction in which the voice is sent.

Without these Foundations your accent will be unfocused and difficult to sustain, but with all four elements working together you will create the solid Foundations on which the rest of the accent is built.

So let's learn how to:

- Feel and sustain the **Setting**.
- Focus the voice in the **Zone**.
- Hear and create the **Tone**.
- Send the voice in the right **Direction**.

...and thereby build your New Standard English Accent's **Foundations**.

THE FOUNDATIONS

In building the Foundations of *any* standard accent the aim is to release the specific muscular tensions that create the overbalances of low or high resonance, nasality, throatiness etc., which give your own regional accent its deliciously quintessential and very recognizable qualities. This is the same for all 'standard' accents, be they Scottish, Welsh, American, Irish or Caribbean.

Releasing the setting, refocusing the zone, balancing the tone, and sending the voice forward, will *automatically* dilute or weaken much of what you think of as your accent, and, to a certain extent, 'standardise' it.

These changes in Foundations are the same processes that young actors go through in the first year of voice training in order to develop their voices and when they often feel they are losing their own accent. Perhaps this is you. In some ways you are changing your accent, as you are changing those very important Foundations, but it is only when you also make changes to the **Shapes** (pages 49-98), the **Bite** (pages 99-132) and the **Groove** (pages 27-40) that you will be speaking with a New Standard English Accent (NSEA).

> *David Tennant (Dr Who, 2005-2010) is an example of an actor who regularly speaks in a Standard Scottish accent, as opposed to his original West Lothian. He has developed standard Foundations which remain the same whether he is speaking Standard Scottish or Standard English. To get back to a fully West Lothian accent those Foundations will be the first thing he changes!*

The Setting

The **setting** of a New Standard English Accent is:

- **Jaw**: Loose and flexible.
- **Cheeks and Lips**: Relaxed and soft, but alert!
- **Tongue**: Tip and blade active, root relaxed and soft.
- **Soft Palate**: Suspended and ready for action. Flexible.

Of course, other accents *sound* different from your own, and one of the factors that creates this difference in sound is a different physical *setting*.

In every accent the muscles of the face and mouth are shaped and held in a particular position: after all, if you ask a mouth to make the same set of moves over and over again it is bound to take up a position that makes those moves as effortless as possible!

Your own articulators (see *Knowing Your Equipment*, page 226) have been moulded over time into their particular setting for *your* own accent. In order

---

to do a New Standard English Accent they will have to break free from that mould and find a *new* setting.

> *We worked with an Australian actress who said that in order to get into the English accent she had to relax her cheek muscles, get a 'scooped-out' feeling in the cheeks, and make a gap between her top and bottom back teeth. These three small adjustments made a huge difference to her setting, making her more able to find and keep her Standard English Accent.*

● **Jaw:** Loose and flexible.

 Feel it: There is a *permanent* space between the teeth, created by release in the muscles of the face that strap round and down from the cheek bones, right under the jaw line. Release in this muscle allows the tone to resonate fully in the oral cavity and for the flesh itself to vibrate.

Drop the jaw and think of opening and creating space in your ears.
Massage and lengthen the 'bulldog' muscle on the side of your face.
Massage away any residual tension in the chin.
Allow the jaw bone to hang freely.

● **Cheeks and Lips:** Relaxed and soft, but alert!

 Feel it: The lip corners and cheeks are relaxed and soft, allowing space in the mouth and encouraging depth in the resonance.

Pinch and stretch the lips with your fingers.
Use your fingers to lift and curl the top lip away from the teeth.
Pout and push the lips forward, then release them.
Try horse blows to release the lips and 'pumpkin' face for the cheeks.

● **Tongue:** The tip and blade active, root relaxed and soft.

 Feel it: The resting position is with the *tip* lying on the floor of the mouth, directly beneath the gum-ridge, with the *centre* of the tongue slightly raised directly under the hard palate.

Hook the tip of your tongue behind your bottom teeth and roll the body forward and out, then allow it to return softly to the centre.
Tap the tip off the gum-ridge: la la la (ta ta ta, da da da).
Let the tongue spring from T to K and build up the pace.

● **Soft Palate:** Suspended and ready for action. Flexible.

 Feel it: The position of this muscle will have a profound effect on the tone of the voice. In Stage Standard English it will be required to bounce up and down depending on the specific speech sound being made. Keep it suspended and ready for action!

See the soft palate lifting up and closing the passageway to your nose by yawning while keeping your tongue flat and forward in your mouth. Make an 'AH' as you do this and feel the sound resonating in the mouth.

See the soft palate drop down and close the passageway to your mouth. Keep your mouth open and say 'NG' (the sound from the end of the word 'sing') and feel the sound resonating in the nose.

To encourage the soft palate to bounce flexibly, switch from the closed 'NG' to the yawned 'AH' sending the 'NG' into the nose and the 'AH' into the mouth. And repeat it!

The Zone

The New Standard English Accent is focused into **Zone 2: The Gum-ridge**

Hear It: Track 3. 'NSEA Zone 2'.

Picture your gum-ridge and the back of your top teeth. Aim the voice forward onto the gum-ridge.

Feel the full effect of the vibrations in this area. Feel the vibrations also pass through the gum-ridge and upper lip and vibrate in the nostrils.

Hear the balance of resonance in this zone.

Each accent has a resonant focal point, or 'placement', in the mouth that we call a **zone**.

Changes in the shaping of the throat and mouth, tongue and soft palate (the setting) affect which zone the voice resonates in. In order to focus your voice into a specific zone, it helps to have a good visual image of the inside of your mouth and to picture the zone you are aiming for.

As you can see in the illustration below there are seven zones, focused on the following areas:

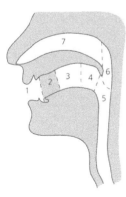

Zone 1: The **Teeth and lips**

Zone 2: The **Gum-ridge**

Zone 3: The **Hard palate**

Zone 4: The **Soft palate** and **uvula**

Zone 5: Down into the **Pharynx** (throat)

Zone 6: Up into the **Naso-pharynx** (behind the nose)

Zone 7: The **Nasal cavity** (right inside and down the nose)

Hear It: *Track 4.* Listen to us focusing a Standard English Accent into each of the seven zones. It only sounds 'neutral' in Zone 2. You will hear how the 'style' of the accent changes from zone to zone. Have a go yourself. Some of the zones may be easier for you to feel and hear than others. Keep working on seeing, hearing and feeling them to really develop sensitivity and flexibility.

See It: Visualise the zones inside your mouth. See your voice travelling and hitting a specific target point in each zone. Do this a few times to get a good sense of each zone. The more you do it, the better you'll get.

Feel It: Feel the vibrations of the voice buzzing in each zone as you focus the sound into it.

Once you have explored all the zones this way, focus specifically on Zone 2. Focusing your sound into this zone is essential for a New Standard English Accent.

> **TOP TIP**
>
> Don't be tempted to raise or lower your pitch as you move into Zone 2: it is the resonance that changes, and not the pitch of the voice.

The Tone

The **tone** of a New Standard English Accent has a woodwind quality, like a clarinet. Words such as velvety, smooth and warm might be used to describe it.

Hear It: *Track 6.*

Changes in the setting and zone directly affect the tone. They can give the tone a greater depth, or make it more lightweight; the tone may seem 'harsher' or 'softer'. What is important is not so much the words that you use to describe it, but your ability to recreate the tone accurately.

Hear It: *Track 5.* Listen to these 3 accents with very differing tonal qualities. These are the words we chose to describe them:

● Manchester – muted trumpet
● Newcastle – owl hooting
● Standard American – brass section

That is what we mean by TONE.

Hear It: Track 6. Listen to these New Standard English Accent speakers. Listen not to *what* they say, but only to the *tone* of their voices, the 'noise' their voices make.

What words would *you* use to describe the tone of these speakers? What musical instruments do they sound like to you? Use these words and instruments to help you establish the tone of this accent.

Direction ─────────────────────

One more thing...

The **direction** of a New Standard English Accent is a wave travelling forward and out of the mouth avoiding all obstacles on the way.

By layering the **setting**, **zone** and **tone** together you have established the essential Foundations of a New Standard English Accent; now to make it come alive you need one more thing: a direction in which to send it.

Not sure what we mean?

When you listen to different accents you may be able to imagine seeing the sound travelling around and out of the mouth in different directions, like arrows. It could be travelling forwards, backwards or even sideways. Listen to these examples and look at the illustration to see and hear what we mean.

See It: and *Hear It: Track 5.*

Listen to these examples and look at the illustrations to hear what we mean.

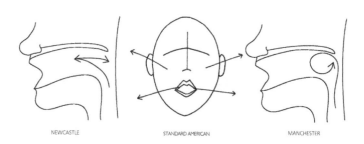

NEWCASTLE   STANDARD AMERICAN   MANCHESTER

As you speak in your New Standard English Accent, establish the direction by imagining you are sending it out of your mouth on a wave like this.

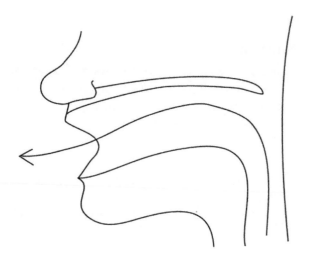

NEW STANDARD ENGLISH ACCENT

And finally...

THE HESITATION SOUND

The New Standard English **hesitation sound** is a slightly forward mid vowel, between the standard DRESS and STRUT vowel.

This little sound can illuminate the Foundations of *any* speaker. The hesitation sound is the sound the mouth makes when it is at its most relaxed, a sort of 'neutral' vowel sound. It is often referred to as schwa (see page 96). You'll hear it a lot when people make a small hesitation sound as they are thinking. You may also hear it on the ends of commA words, and also lettER words in a Non-Rhotic accent (see page 95). It can change subtly or dramatically from one accent to another. Knowing and keeping the right hesitation sound is a good way of keeping the accent in your mouth even when you are NOT speaking, as well as when you are!

Hear It – other accents: Track 7. Listen to all these hesitation sounds... You can hear how different they can be from one accent to another!

Hear It: Track 8. Now listen to this New Standard English Accent hesitation sound.

To be sure that your New Standard English Accent Foundations are in place, listen to the hesitation sound on the MP3 and check yours against it. If the hesitation sound is wrong it is a clear indicator that something in the Foundations is not quite right!

THE FOUNDATIONS CHECKLIST

NSEA

- **The Setting:**

    Jaw: Loose and flexible.

    Cheeks and Lips: Relaxed and soft, but alert!

    Tongue: Tip and blade active, root relaxed and soft.

    Soft Palate: Suspended and ready for action. Flexible.

- **The Zone:** 2 (gum-ridge).
- **The Tone:** woodwind quality; velvety, smooth and warm.
- **The Direction:** a wave travelling forward and out of the mouth avoiding all obstacles on the way.
- **The Hesitation Sound:** a slightly forward mid vowel, between DRESS and STRUT vowels.

YOU

- What is the muscular **Setting** of your accent?
- What **Zone** is your accent focused in?
- What does the **Tone** of your accent sound like?
- What **Direction** does your accent travel in?
- What **Hesitation Sound** does your accent make?

Put your observations in the 'Foundations' section of the **You and the New** chart at www.howtodoaccents.com.

2

THE GROOVE

IN THIS CHAPTER...

We will explore the 'Groove' of a New Standard English Accent. Every accent has its own music, made from a complex interplay of rhythms and tunes. Think how speech would sound without music: robotic, just data, empty words. Whenever you listen to someone speak, whatever their accent, you are hearing three things: *words*, which express literal meaning, *rhythm* which focuses you on specific syllables, and *tune*, which provides the all important emotional or subtextual meaning. It is the rhythm and tune that are the focus of this chapter.

When learning a new Groove first get **The Big Picture**:

- **Frame it:**
  Put the cultural, historical and geographical frame around your Groove to understand where it comes from.

- **Embody it:**
  Feel the new Groove in your voice and body.
  Play the Laban Action.

- **Identify the Default Tune:**
  Identify three characteristics of a neutral statement:
  Laban Action
  Default Tune
  Musical Quality

Then add **The Detail**:

- **Intonation:**
  Refine your ability to listen to and recreate specific intonation patterns. Learn the new ryhthms and six basic tune possibilities of a NSEA.

- **Owning it:**
  Connect to the actions and intentions behind these rhythms and tunes. Explore our Top Ten broad, but really useful, launch and land combinations.

There are two important points to bear in mind as an actor when exploring new Grooves.

The Groove is one of the first things, as babies, that we learn, not just how to do it but also how to interpret it emotionally. Then as we grow and develop our own life story, our Grooves resound with our personal cultural, historical and geographical legacies. This can make changing the Groove trickier than you might expect. There can be strong identity issues at stake. We may hold on strongly to our own music; after all, it is how we express the emotions, intentions and feelings that lie underneath our words. Be aware of this, and recognise that this is true for your character too. That this is their own Groove, as much as yours is your own.

Secondly, our own emotional interpretations may lead to misunderstandings or judgements of certain tunes and rhythms. A neutral tune that is quite innocent or matter-of-fact in a Standard English accent may be far from neutral in your own. You may even feel uncomfortable using it. It is important to recognise your responses, and use them initially if they help you find the Groove, but be sure to remove the mistaken judgement from them and connect to the true meaning and impulses behind them.

How To Do Standard English Accents

THE BIG PICTURE

As a general description of this particular Groove, the music of a New Standard English Accent is more expansive and broad than some of the varieties we explore in the second half of the book. It moves up and down the vertical, rather than pushing along the horizontal. The voice tends to spring off the consonants to drive the phrase, and there is a strong preference for the use of range rather than volume to stress words or clarify expression. The weight focuses heavily on one *key* Landing Point in the phrase, the momentum launching you to that point, with airy lightness on the journey.

Hear It: Track 2. Listen to these speakers talking freely on their own subjects. Notice your responses to the Groove they use; get a feel for it, mimic and 'sing along' if you feel like it, and listen again whenever you need to.

2

Frame it

In a sense, because this is a 'standard' accent, there are no specific frames. After all, the whole point of a standard accent is that it should contain no cultural, historical or geographical information! A full cultural, historical and geographical frame can only really be created as you learn about the world of your specific play or character.

But of course, as you read in **Get Into the Scene** (see pages 9-11), this accent was born of the Received Pronunciation of the first half of the 20th century, which in turn was born of the accent of the upper classes, and so the cultural, historical and geographical influences on those accents frame this one, to a certain extent, too. For example, the open spaces, mixed landscapes and varied geographical environments that were the nurseries of RP, could be said to give rise to the expansive and broad use of range; the lack of time pressure and the relatively quiet environments could also give the voice the physical freedom to use range as the expressive tool, as there is little need to use tension and volume and push. There can be a quickness and momentum that drives to the key Landing Point, matching the expressive language of the classics and the enjoyment of the art of the debate. Also vigorous sports like horse riding and its associated activities such as hunting and jumping may be heard in the pace, muscularity and potential for dramatic leaps.

The other important frame around the Groove of this accent is of course the cultural and historical legacies of voice training for the actor. The aim of voice training is to open up the actor's voice beyond the limits of habit, to give them the freedom to express the thoughts, feelings and motivations of Hamlet, Antigone, Phaedre, etc., without imposing their own specific cultural or geographic limitations on them, and in a way that is accessible to a very wide and varied audience. This applies not just to the articulation of thought through speech sounds, but to the expression of meaning through music.

> *The speaker's desire to animate his listener should compel his attention to his instrument for doing so.*
>
> Gwyneth L. Thurburn, *Voice and Speech*, 1939.

Embody it

Different Grooves have different energies, dynamics and momentums.

In order to explore a Groove successfully we have found that nothing beats getting physical. The body has an instinct for rhythm and tune that your mind may struggle to interpret. The voice likes to take its lead from the actions of the body. If you want to speak in a new Groove, move your body in that Groove and the voice will follow.

Actions derived from sports and dance – or other physical movements such as floating, punching, swinging, etc. – have often helped us to get a Groove into an actor's body, which in turn has helped them to understand and, more importantly, internalise the momentum and music of an accent.

Hear It: *Track 9.* Listen to this excerpt from *Arthur the Rat* 'spoken' using only the Groove.

Feel It: What does this Groove feel like physically? What physicality would you instinctively add?

- An orangutan swinging through trees…?
- Rhythmic gymnastics…?
- Smooth ice skating…?

One old-school classic for teaching a Standard English Accent Groove is the chiffon scarf exercise…easily replicated with a sheet of toilet roll ten squares long!

Feel It: Holding one end of the scarf, and using your whole arm from the shoulder, draw a full figure of 8 on its side in the air in front of you with the scarf.

Let your knees bend as the scarf hits the centre of the 8.

Let the end of the scarf float freely while the momentum of your hand aims towards the centre of the 8.

Now use the text below. The chiffon scarf must hit the centre of the 8 on the marked stressed syllables and glide through the air on the unmarked, unstressed syllables.

There was **once** a young **rat** named **Ar**thur, who could **never** take the **trouble** to **make** up his **mind**!

See It: One of the most important features of all varieties of Standard English accents is the balance of stressed and unstressed syllables. The syllables speed up when unstressed, as the chiffon scarf glides through the air…and slow down when stressed, as the chiffon hits the centre point.

The movement of the chiffon scarf, gliding lightly but with direction, and with the impetus and momentum heading to the centre point of the 8, mimics the rhythms of a New Standard English Accent Groove.

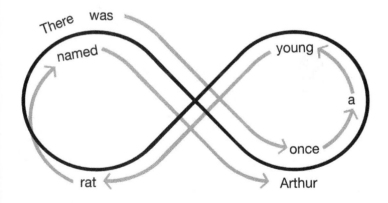

Another great way of getting the Groove into your voice and body is to use a simple system of physical dynamics. Fortunately for us a movement expert called Rudolf Laban devised a system for understanding the way in which a movement is performed! Laban identified three elements with contrasting polar opposites: space, weight and time.

		SPACE	WEIGHT	TIME
	GLIDE	Direct	Light	Sustained
	FLOAT	Indirect	Light	Sustained
	DAB	Direct	Light	Sudden
	FLICK	Indirect	Light	Sudden
	PRESS	Direct	Heavy	Sustained
	WRING	Indirect	Heavy	Sustained
	PUNCH	Direct	Heavy	Sudden
	SLASH	Indirect	Heavy	Sudden

The New Standard English Accent uses GLIDE as the overall dynamic, with DAB for the unstressed syllables

Hear It: *Track 10.* Listen to this excerpt from *Arthur the Rat* 'spoken' using the actions of Dab and Glide.

Feel It: Try using the action of Dab and Glide as you read *Arthur the Rat* (see page 225).

This is by no means saying that the New Standard English Accent ONLY uses Dab and Glide. What it is saying is that this is the *emotionally neutral* Groove. You could think of it as the 'newsreader' Groove; a Groove with no added meaning or subtext, which is an important starting point as it may be very different from your own.

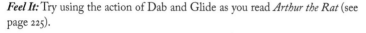

Once you can confidently use these 'emotionally neutral' dynamics, try changing the Laban Action to allow other feelings and subtexts to come into play. This will develop your accent to allow you to express the actions, intentions and emotional journey of any character.

Hear It: *Track 11.* Listen to these examples of a NSEA spoken using other Laban Actions. What subtextual feelings or actions do they suggest?

How To Identify the Default Tune

One way of comparing and contrasting accents is to identify the intonation used to make a *basic statement*, with no subtextual meaning or implication. We call this the **Default Tune**. It will have three qualities:

- **Laban Action**
- an **over and down** or **under and up** pattern
- a **Musical Quality**

This gives you the basic tune against which all the other musical possibilities will be played.

Hear It: *Track 12.* Listen to the intonation used by a Liverpool Accent and a New Standard English Accent to make this basic statement, with no subtextual meaning or implication:

Susan bought a sandwich for me.

In Laban Action terms we say NSEA uses Dab and Glide. We might describe a Liverpool Accent, in contrast, as using Wring.

Now listen again to the way the tune moves.

The Liverpool Accent starts relatively high, travels **down** and then rises **up** again. We would call this an **under and up** Default Tune.

The NSEA starts relatively low, travels **up** and then falls **down** again. We would call this an **over and down** Default Tune.

See It:

Liverpool: Under and Up	NSEA: Over and Down

Finally you can describe the **Musical Quality.** If you were to write a piece of music that sounded like the accent, would you write it in a major or minor key? We would describe a Liverpool Accent as having a **minor** quality and a NSEA as having a **major** quality.

Hear It: Track 12.

Now when you listen to this default statement in a New Standard English Accent you can identify three broad Groove characteristics:

Laban Action: Dab and Glide

Default Tune: Over and Down

Musical Quality: Major

> TOP TIP
>
> Actors beware! This only establishes the **Default Tune.** How often are Hamlet or Mascha or Hedda likely to choose the default as their tool of expression? The Groove of the New Standard English Accent will of course slash and punch, have minor keys, go under and up, all in response to shifts in impulses and intentions. What it clearly gives you is a strong indicator of how close to, or far from, a New Standard English Accent, your own accent's Default Tune is.

THE DETAIL

Intonation

Whenever you listen to someone speak, whatever their accent, you hear three things: **words**, which express literal meaning, **rhythm** which focuses you on specific syllables, and **tune**, which provides the emotional or subtextual meaning.

The specific combination of rhythm and tune across a phrase of speech is what we call **Intonation**.

Hear It: Track 13.

- **Words**… This is just the words, you can hear the shapes and bite. Some of the accent is there but something's missing…

- **+ Rhythm**… Now I've added the rhythm so you know which bits to focus on, but it still doesn't sound quite right… I sound a bit like a robot… There's one more thing to add…

- **+ Tune**… And that's the tune. The words, rhythm and tune combined are what make intonation. With all three things together, you have the whole accent!

Listening to and mimicking these combinations accurately is a vital skill to develop in order to do *any* accent. In this section we will pick apart some of the *main* patterns used in a New Standard English Accent. But remember, to really be able to 'play' the intonation fluently, it is important to immerse yourself in the music, listening, learning and responding to the emotions and intentions conveyed. So let's begin to:

- Refine the rhythm and tune.
- Connect to the intention.

The Rhythm

Landing Points

Whatever tune you use on the **Landing Point** will have the greatest effect on the meaning – so what is a Landing Point and how do you find it? Put simply, the Landing Point is the last stressed syllable in a chunk, or phrase.

For example in the following phrase:

Susan bought a sandwich for me.

The stressed *syllables* could be:

Susan **bought** a **sand**wich for me.

and the Landing Point would be **sand**.

...the launch begins on the syllable *Su*...

...the tune journeys through *san **bought** a* to get to...

...the Landing Point **sand**...

...then tails off into *wich for me.*

So in this phrase, whatever tune you use on the syllable **sand** will have the greatest effect on the meaning.

The Tune

There are **six basic tune** possibilities for the **Landing Point** in a phrase which you will find useful to familiarise yourself with. We will deal with their possible meanings and implications later. For now, copy what you hear as we go through it to train your ear and your voice.

See It and *Hear It: Track 14.*

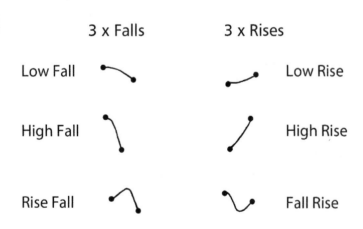

Hear It: *Track 15.* Now listen to these used in a phrase:

Low Fall

sand   **sand**wich   Susan bought a **sand**wich   Susan bought a **sand**wich for me

High Fall

sand   **sand**wich   Susan bought a **sand**wich   Susan bought a **sand**wich for me

Rise Fall

sand   **sand**wich   Susan bought a **sand**wich   Susan bought a **sand**wich for me

Low Rise

sand   **sand**wich   Susan bought a **sand**wich   Susan bought a **sand**wich for me

High Rise

sand   **sand**wich   Susan bought a **sand**wich   Susan bought a **sand**wich for me

Fall Rise

sand   **sand**wich   Susan bought a **sand**wich   Susan bought a **sand**wich for me

Hear It: *Track 16.* Now listen to these four basic sentence types, where there is no extra subtextual meaning or implication, with the Landing Point still on the word 'sandwich'. These are the Default Tunes used for these sentence types:

Sentence Type		Default Tune
Statement	Susan bought a sandwich for me.	Low Fall or High Fall
Why question	Why did she buy you a sandwich?	Low Fall or High Fall
Yes/No question	Did she buy you a sandwich?	Low Rise or High Rise
Command	Buy me a sandwich!	Low Fall or High Fall

Clearly, the tune is not all in the **Landing Point**; how you *launch* the phrase to get to the **Landing Point** can subtly alter the tune and therefore the meaning. So now let's look at some combinations and their meanings...

Owning It

If you are really unfamiliar with the intonation of a New Standard English Accent, or your own intonation is very different, the following ten patterns are really worth practising. Of course, the reality of intonation is that there are infinite combinations, reflecting the infinitely subtle differences of each individual and their meanings, actions and intentions. These ten examples are merely a starting point...

Ten Broad But Really Useful Launch and Land Combinations

 Hear It: Track 17.

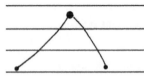

1. Low Launch to a High Fall Personal concern, excitement, protesting or impatient:

Statement: Susan bought a sandwich for me.
Why question: Why did she buy you a sandwich?
Yes/No question: Did she buy you a sandwich?
Command: Buy me a sandwich!

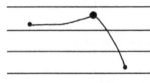

2. High Launch to High Fall Warm, gentle suggestion (lacks any protest/impatience of the previous example):

Statement: Susan bought a sandwich for me.
Why question: Why did she buy you a sandwich?
Yes/No question: Did she buy you a sandwich?
Command: Buy me a sandwich!

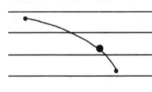

3. High Launch to Low Fall Categoric, weighty, serious, intense:

Statement: Susan bought a sandwich for me.
Why question: Why did she buy you a sandwich?
Yes/No question: Did she buy you a sandwich?
Command: Buy me a sandwich!

4. Low Launch to Low Fall Cool, phlegmatic, detatched, dull:

Statement: Susan bought a sandwich for me.
Why question: Why did she buy you a sandwich?
Yes/No question: Did she buy you a sandwich?
Command: Buy me a sandwich!

5. Low Launch to High Rise Incomplete, non-critical questioning, tentative, turns commands into requests and statements into questions:

Statement: Susan bought a sandwich for me.
Why question: Why did she buy you a sandwich?
Yes/No question: Did she buy you a sandwich?
Command: Buy me a sandwich!

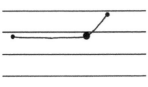

6. **High Launch to High Rise** As 5 but even softer and gentler:

Statement: Susan bought a sandwich for me.
Why question: Why did she buy you a sandwich?
Yes/No question: Did she buy you a sandwich?
Command: Buy me a sandwich!

7. **Low Launch to Low Rise** Invites further contribution, reserves judgement, sceptical, reproving:

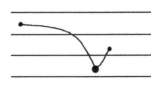

Statement: Susan bought a sandwich for me.
Why question: Why did she buy you a sandwich?
Yes/No question: Did she buy you a sandwich?
Command: Buy me a sandwich!

8. **High Launch to Low Rise** Soothing, reassuring, confident, can also therefore be patronising and irritating. With yes/no questions it is the default:

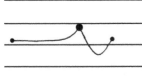

Statement: Susan bought a sandwich for me.
Why question: Why did she buy you a sandwich?
Yes/No question: Did she buy you a sandwich?
Command: Buy me a sandwich!

In these next and final two examples how you launch is not important, the subtextual implications in the bending tones on the landing are overwhelming!

9. **Fall Rise** Tentative, non-finality, something implied but not said, speaker has reservations:

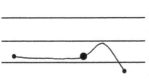

Statement: Susan bought a sandwich for me.
Why question: Why did she buy you a sandwich?
Yes/No question: Did she buy you a sandwich?
Command: Buy me a sandwich!

10. **Rise Fall** Impressed, challenging, antagonistic, disclaiming responsibility:

Statement: Susan bought a sandwich for me.
Why question: Why did she buy you a sandwich?
Yes/No question: Did she buy you a sandwich?
Command: Buy me a sandwich!

THE GROOVE CHECKLIST

NSEA

- **Laban Action:** GLIDE and DAB.
- **Default Tune:** Over and down.
- **Musical Quality:** Major.

YOU

- Which **Laban Action** most closely matches your accent?
- Does your **Default Tune** go over and down, or under and up?
- Is the **Musical Quality** of your accent major or minor?

3

THE TWO PLANETS

IN THIS CHAPTER...

When it comes to accents the world divides into two planets:

Rhotic – People who always say an 'R' whenever it is written.

> right √ harry √ bring √ hero √
> here √ cart √ mother √

Non-Rhotic – People who only say an 'R' if there is a vowel sound spoken after it:

> right √ harry √ bring √ hero √
> here x cart x mother x

ALL varieties of Standard English Accents live on Planet Non-Rhotic.

So what planet is your accent on, and can you learn the rules to pass as a local on planet Non-Rhotic?

Look at the phrase: 'Law and Order'.

How many 'Rs' do you see? Two!

Now speak it out loud: 'Law and Order'.

How many 'Rs' do you say?

- Some of you will be saying two 'Rs', both in the word Order: if so, **your accent is Rhotic**

- Some of you will be saying no 'Rs' at all, while others of you may be saying one 'R', and you'll be saying it where there isn't even one written, like this: 'law r-and awduh': if so, **your accent is Non-Rhotic.**

And to make doubly sure:

Say the name of this letter the way you normally would when reciting the alphabet:

'R'

Do you feel your tongue move to shape an 'R'? Then **your accent is Rhotic**.

Does it stay flat, making an 'AH'? Then **your accent is Non-Rhotic**.

That's what we mean by different planets!

If your own accent is Rhotic, the Non-Rhotic patterns can present some interesting challenges, and it will be vital that you read, absorb and practise the following chapter.

Even if your own accent is Non-Rhotic, it is still not all plain sailing. Jump to **How To Do 'R'** (page 44).

Planet Non-Rhotic

ALL varieties of Standard English Accents live on Planet Non-Rhotic. They are what we call Non-Rhotic accents. On Planet Non-Rhotic there are two rules:

Only ever say an 'R' if it is followed by a vowel sound.

Never say an 'R' if it is followed by a consonant.

See It:

Look at this word: *Cargo*
Although there's an 'R' written, it's followed by a consonant, so don't say it!

And this word: *Order*
There are two 'Rs' written here; the first 'R' is followed by a consonant ('d') and the second 'R' ends the word, so don't say them!

Now look at this word: *Hero*
This 'R' is followed by a vowel sound, so do say it!

And what about this word? *Hairy*
Although the 'Y' looks like a consonant it is spoken here as a vowel sound, meaning this 'R' is followed by a vowel, so do say it!

And these teasers? *Here   Care*
It may look like the 'R' is followed by a vowel, but it isn't a spoken vowel so bang goes the 'R': don't say it!

How to DROP 'R' on Planet Non-Rhotic ─────

Hear It: *Track 18.*

Listen to this NSEA speaker saying the following words without pronouncing the 'Rs':

Park   Stern   Court

Here   There   Pure

Poor   Hair   Ear

Water   Mother   Actor

Feel It:

- Say the words yourself, losing the 'Rs' completely.
- Instead of an 'R', lengthen the vowel.
- Keep the tip of your tongue behind your bottom teeth during the vowel.

See It:

Look in the mirror. Check that you are not contracting any muscles for that non-existent 'R'.

Be careful: your tongue may think it's not doing an 'R', and maybe it doesn't sound like an 'R' to you, but is your tongue still moving? Even a little bit? Even the slightest movement of the tongue, however small, will still be heard as an 'R' by a Non-Rhotic speaker. It really does need to be dropped completely. Watch your lip muscles too. These need only shape the vowel, not the 'R'!

Now practise this little sentence. Remember the rule: if it's followed by a spoken vowel sound you say it; if it's not you don't!

> Margaret, Rhys and Richard poured water all over the flowers; they loved pouring water.

TOP TIP

We have found that it can really help Rhotic people to rewrite the words without an 'R' in the spelling, and to see the words this way:

Mahgret pawed the watuh, Richud loved flowuh powuh

How to DO 'R' on Planet Non-Rhotic

Non-Rhotic 'R' is only said when followed by a vowel sound. It is no longer just a letter in a word, it has a special job to do: it's a springboard off which the next vowel can jump, giving a bounce to the start of syllables.

The result is these three potential features of Non-Rhotic accents:

● The mid-word bounce (see below): Gerry = Ge–rry

● The linking bounce (page 45): *Car alarm* = Ca–ralarm

● The intrusive bounce (page 46): *Linda and I* = Linda–rand I

The linking and intrusive bounces are only ever used in rapid, flowing speech. When the pace slows down, those 'Rs' disappear. And although the linking bounce is a feature of *all* styles and varieties of Standard English Accent, the intrusive bounce has issues!

The mid-word bounce

On Planet Non-Rhotic the 'R' is used to bounce into the next syllable.

Hear It: *Track 19.*

Look at these words with 'R' in the middle and listen to our New Standard English Accent speakers say them:

Very   Sorry   Harry   Worry   Spirit   Courage

See It:

The syllables are clearly separated. The vowel before the 'R' must be kept absolutely clean of any influence from the 'R' that follows it!

Ve–ry   So–rry   Ha–rry   Wo–rry   Spi–rit   Cou–rage

Feel It:

If your own accent is Rhotic, you may make your 'R' part of the first syllable, resulting in the 'R' merging with the preceding vowel. The two syllables seem to glide into one another, like this:

Ver–y   Sorr–y   Harr–y   Worr–y   Spir–it   Cour–age

Speak the example words yourself slowly and carefully, feeling the separation of the syllables, keeping the 'R' clear of the preceding vowel and using the 'R' to bounce into the following syllable.

Ve–ry   So–rry   Ha–rry   Wo–rry   Spi–rit   Cou–rage

The linking bounce

Hear It: *Track 20.*

Listen to this NSEA speaker. They are using the 'R' as a linking bounce.

Car	Cah ralahm
More	Maw rovuh
Here	Hea rl am

When an 'R' ends a word a Non-Rhotic speaker won't say it because it's not followed by a spoken vowel:

Car   More   Here

However, if the next word starts with a vowel...then the 'R' has its job back!

The Non-Rhotic speaker 'links' the two words with the 'R'. (Watch out! This won't happen if the speaker breaks the flow or breathes between the words!)

Cah ralahm   Maw rovuh   Hea rl am

Feel It:

First say the word on its own without the 'R':

Car   More   Here

Now put the words together using a very soft 'R' to start the following word without breaking the flow:

Cah ralahm   Maw rovuh   Hea rl am

Now practise with this little phrase. We have marked the linking bounces:

John tipped watuh rinto the plants, maw rover Wilbuh rand Linda didn't!

The intrusive bounce

And here's the final and somewhat cheeky little bounce…

On Planet Non-Rhotic, just because there's no 'R' written, it doesn't mean you can't do one. Some Non-Rhotics just hate having two vowel sounds next to each other. They feel they just have to insert a consonant to help with the flow! For some Non-Rhotic speakers, it can feel entirely natural to insert an 'R' to make a cheeky little bounce from one vowel to another!

Edda and Jan = 'Edda rand Jan'.

This is often referred to as an intrusive 'R', because the sound of an 'R' intrudes where there is no written 'R'. But remember, it only ever happens when speech is rapid and flowing!

Although it is a natural feature of many Non-Rhotic accents, when it comes to New Standard English Accent there are issues.

In a New Standard English Accent the intrusive bounce is:

- **Often used between words**, after the commA and THOUGHT vowels. When this happens it should be **extremely** light and gentle and almost imperceptible.

India rand China   Linda ris   Draw rout

- **Not used in the middle of words** with the THOUGHT vowel (though in many regional accents it is!):

Pawing   Drawing

If you are naturally Rhotic this feature may feel bizarre, and, as it was traditionally frowned upon by elocution teachers in the past, feel free not to use it at all!

If you are naturally Non-Rhotic, however (e.g. London, Manchester, Boston, New York City), you may need to fight powerful urges to use your heavyweight intrusive bounces everywhere! Practise eradicating them completely in the middle of words such as PAWING and DRAWING, then soften those heavy ones between words.

3

PLANET NON-RHOTIC CHECKLIST

When it comes to knowing when the New Standard English Accent uses an **R** remember:

- **Only say an 'R' if the next sound is a vowel:** Hero   Very   Married
- **Never say an 'R' if the next sound is a consonant or if it ends a word:**
  Cargo   Park   Car   Here
- **Remember your linking bounces:** Cah ralahm   Maw rovuh   Hea rl am
- **Never use an intrusive bounce in the middle of a word:**
  Drawing   Pawing
- **Keep the intrusive bounces light and gentle between words:**
  Edda rand Jan   Law rand order

4

THE SHAPES

IN THIS CHAPTER...

We will
- Give you the Tools and Skills you need for shaping vowels
- Show you how to do each of the vowel shapes used in a NSEA
- Take you through some key Environmental Issues

Although there are 24 *possible* vowel sets in accents of English, in a **New Standard English Accent** some of these sets have *merged*, so that there are just **eighteen** separate sets.

Each set has its own vowel shape and a key word (or words). The word KIT, for example, represents a set of all the words that use the same vowel shape as that found in the word KIT, such as ship, bridge, myth and busy.

The eighteen vowel shapes of a New Standard English Accent are (merged sets are in brackets):

1. KIT - page 54
2. DRESS - page 56
3. STRUT - page 58
4. FOOT - page 60
5. GOOSE - page 62
6. FLEECE - page 64
7. NURSE - page 66
8. TRAP - page 68
9. BATH (PALM-START) - **page 70**
10. LOT (CLOTH) - **page 72**
11. THOUGHT (NORTH-FORCE-TOUR) - **page 74**
12. FACE - page 76
13. GOAT - page 78
14. PRICE - page 80
15. CHOICE - page 82
16. MOUTH - page 84
17. NEAR - page 86
18. SQUARE - page 88

We will tell you:
- How to make each shape
- Whether it is short or long
- Whether it is steady or sliding

We will also explore the issues around each shape:
- Alert you to the most common mistakes
- Give you top tips on how to get it right!

And because 'no vowel is an island' we will also take you through some of the key **Environmental Issues**, looking at how vowels may behave differently depending on the consonants or other vowels that surround them.

NB. It is important to point out that the descriptions we give are for a *New* Neutral Standard English Accent. Some of the shapes have changed *considerably* from those that are often described in voice training manuals of the last century. The most significant changes are in the TRAP, GOOSE, FOOT, SQUARE and TOUR shapes. For an overview of the Old Stage Standard Accent, see pages 129-132.

TOOLS AND SKILLS FOR SHAPING VOWELS...

One of the most important skills is knowing how to use the Kit List.

Hear It: Track 21.

Listen to the Kit List being read by these New Standard English Accent speakers. Listen to it once and do nothing, just listen!

KIT	**NURSE**	**GOAT**
DRESS	**TRAP**	**PRICE**
STRUT	**BATH–PALM–START**	**CHOICE**
FOOT	**LOT–CLOTH**	**MOUTH**
GOOSE	**THOUGHT–NORTH–FORCE (TOUR)**	**NEAR**
FLEECE	**FACE**	**SQUARE**

Hear It and *Feel It: Track 21.* Listen to it again and this time, mimic what you hear, repeating each word after you hear it, using your **funnel** to hear yourself clearly.

Write down anything you notice, make a note of any surprising sounds. Pay attention to those shapes which are:

- Unexpected
- Different from yours
- Similar, but not quite the same

Make a note of these and work on these first.

As you work on each vowel shape we will be encouraging you to use the following Tools and Skills:

SEEING A MAP

See It:

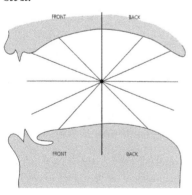

Having a visual map of where the vowel 'sits' in your mouth and in relation to other vowels can really help. Imagine this is a map of the inside of your mouth, seen from the side, and divided into segments.

Some vowels will be at the front, some at the back, some in the middle, and some will slide from one place to another, depending on the shape of the tongue and lips.

4

HEARING A WHISPER

Hear It: *Track 22.*

Edda is whispering a specific vowel shape. Listen to Jan as she plays with various whispered shapes until she finds the same one. Try tuning in yourself, using your funnel (see page 12).

Shaping vowels on a *whisper* means you can really pay attention to the shape and its resonance and not be distracted by your voice.

Depending on the shape of the vowel and where it 'sits' on the map the resonance will be anything from very high (FLEECE) to very low (THOUGHT). Those at the front will have a higher resonance, those at the back will have a lower resonance.

Hear It: Make a selection of your own whispered shapes and use your funnel to listen to them.

FEELING A SHAPE

Feel It:

See It:

Jaw position: We will be referring to three jaw positions: 1 (neutral), 2 and 3.

Position 1	Position 2	Position 3

 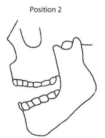 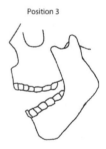

 See It:

Tongue Shape: The tongue shape is possibly the most important of all in getting the vowel right, but being on the inside of you it can be tricky to know what it's doing!

The tongue humps up to create a vowel shape. If it humps at the front the vowel will have a higher resonant quality, at the back it has a lower resonant quality.

The tongue is attached to the jaw. As well as making its own independent shapes, as the jaw opens and closes through positions 1-3 the hump will be closer or further away from the roof of the mouth.

See It:

Lip and Cheek Shape: Lips and cheeks are responsible for a significant amount of the resonant quality of a vowel. They can lengthen or shorten the oral chamber, and pick up or muffle the overtones in the sound. Wide thin lips pick up high frequencies, while round plump lips pick up low ones. Make the following shapes with your mouth on a whisper and hear the note change with each lip shape:

4

> **TOP TIP**
>
> Remember the Foundations? Get these right and many of the vowels will take care of themselves. With the shift in setting, zone and tone they will change automatically, leaving you free to focus on those that are more of a stretch.

As a baby you dedicated hours to hearing the sounds around you, playing with the shape of your mouth, until the sounds *you* were making matched the sounds you were *hearing* and/or *seeing*. You then practised those shapes and movements over and over again until they became *locked* into your muscle memory. Time to unlock your old muscle memories and create new ones…

How To Do Standard English Accents

HOW TO DO...THE KIT VOWEL SHAPE

Length: **SHORT**

Movement: **STEADY**

Hear It: Track 23.

The ship listed as busy women built a pretty bridge in the dim mid-winter.

See It: Illustration + mirror

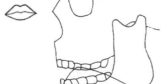

Feel It:

Jaw: **Position 1.**

Tongue: **The hump is forward and high, slightly back from the gum-ridge.**

Lips/Cheeks: **Lips a *tiny* bit spread.**

Map/Resonance: **This vowel sits almost at the front high point on the map. The resonance is at the front and has a high quality.**

NOT GOT IT YET?

Hear It: Track 23 + Funnel.

Listen again to the whispered vowel shape.

It is important that you can hear the resonant quality of the *shape*, not your voice. If you have the right shape, the resonant note will match the one on the MP3. Bingo!

In order to hear the resonant note of the *shape* without the distraction of your voice, whisper the shape with *air only*, and use your funnel. It helps to put a slight 'H' before it.

- Listen to the 'note' that is produced by the **shape** as you whisper air through it.
- Compare the note to the one on the MP3 and by subtly changing tongue and lip position, get the notes to match.
- Try sliding from the schwa (see page 96) up to the 'EE', or back from the 'EE' to the schwa on a whisper and stopping when you hear the 'I' of KIT.
- When you are sure that your shape and note match the one on the MP3, add voice to the shape as you breathe out, first on one sustained note, then in your 'spoken' voice.

For other examples of words using this shape go to KIT in the Kit List sets at www.howtodoaccents.com

NB. Along with the commA–lettER vowel or schwa (see page 96), the KIT vowel is the vowel that a New Standard English Accent often uses in unstressed syllables, in words such as **wanted, married, nurses, erroneous**. Now that you are familiar with the shape and sound of this vowel, try it in the unstressed syllables in the following sentences:

> Yvonne wanted to invite the beloved dictator. Imagine such irrational behaviour. Remember enough information to eradicate the emotive debate.
> His friends were spirited, and interested in the illegal ragged and crooked Rinaldo.

COMMON MISTAKES

Too wide: The lips and tongue spread tightly, killing some of the lower resonances and giving a thin, reedy quality to the vowel. Practise in the mirror, and check that you are not over-tensing the lips as you make this sound.

Too long: A slight stretch on this vowel can send it to Essex. Keep it short and snappy!

Too flat: The tongue flattens towards the DRESS vowel, or the schwa. Keep it tight and bright!

EE/I: Some languages don't have a distinction between a FLEECE-like vowel and a KIT-like vowel, making FIT and FEET sound the same! If this is you, look at the FLEECE description and use these pairs of words to help you distinguish:

FIT FEET PITTA PETER LIP LEAP KIPPER KEEPER BIT BEET MIT MEET (etc.)

TOP TIPS FOR NORTH AMERICANS

Watch out for any tendency to lengthen the vowel and slide to a neutral position. Keep it high, short and steady!

HOW TO DO...THE DRESS VOWEL SHAPE

Length: **SHORT**

Movement: **STEADY**

Hear It: Track 24.

In a sweat, Jeff edged his head into the Thames in an effort to save his best friend from the treacherous bell of death.

See It: Illustration + mirror

Feel It:

Jaw: **Position 2.**

Tongue: **The hump is slightly forward from the midpoint.**

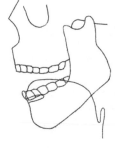

Lips/Cheeks: **Lips a *tiny* bit spread.**

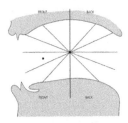

Map/Resonance: **This vowel sits close to the midline at the front on the map. The resonance is at the front and has a mid to high quality.**

NOT GOT IT YET?

Hear It: Track 24 + Funnel.

Listen again to the whispered vowel shape.

It is important that you can hear the resonant quality of the *shape*, not your voice. If you have the right shape, the resonant note will match the one on the MP3. Bingo!

In order to hear the resonant note of the *shape* without the distraction of your voice, whisper the shape with *air only*, and use your funnel. It helps to put a slight 'H' before it.

● Listen to the 'note' that is produced by the *shape* as you whisper air through it.

● Compare the note to the one on the MP3 and by subtly changing tongue and lip position, get the notes to match.

● Drop the jaw open to just beyond the neutral setting, allowing even more space for the body of the tongue to roll forward. With the tip behind the bottom teeth, roll the body of the tongue forward very gently.

● When you are sure that your shape and note match the one on the MP3, add voice to the shape as you breathe out, first on one note, then in your 'spoken' voice.

For other examples of words using this shape go to DRESS in the Kit List sets at www.howtodoaccents.com

COMMON MISTAKES

Too far back, and close to the TRAP: Losing the brightness of the sound.

● Place your tongue in the FLEECE vowel shape.

● Hold the tongue in this rolled forward shape as you slowly open the jaw to position 2, allowing the tongue to move with it, without letting it flatten!

● Breathe out on a whisper as you do this, until you hear the New Standard English 'E' of DRESS.

TOP TIPS FOR NORTH AMERICANS

Keep the sound forward and bright, as above. Watch out for any tendency to lengthen and slide to schwa. Keep it short and keep it steady!

HOW TO DO...THE STRUT VOWEL SHAPE

Length: **SHORT**

Movement: **STEADY**

Hear It: Track 25.

The dull young monks rushed in a flood to hunt the buds of the lovely buttercup.

See It: Illustration + mirror

Feel It:

Jaw: **Position 3.**

Tongue: **Neutral and relaxed (the hump will sit just below the centre of the mouth).**

Lips/Cheeks: **Neutral and relaxed.**

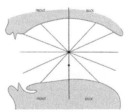

Map/Resonance: This vowel sits in the middle of the map, just below the centre point. The resonance is in the middle and has a mid-note quality.

NOT GOT IT YET?

Hear It: Track 25 + Funnel.

Listen again to the whispered vowel shape.

It is important that you can hear the resonant quality of the *shape*, not your voice. If you have the right shape, the resonant note will match the one on the MP3. Bingo!

In order to hear the resonant note of the *shape* without the distraction of your voice, whisper the shape with *air only*, and use your funnel. It helps to put a slight 'H' before it.

- Listen to the 'note' that is produced by the *shape* as you whisper air through it.

- Compare the note to the one on the MP3 and by subtly changing tongue and lip position, get the notes to match.

- When you are sure that your shape and note match the one on the MP3, add voice to the shape as you breathe out, first on one note, then in your 'spoken' voice.

For other examples of words using this shape go to STRUT in the Kit List sets at www.howtodoaccents.com

COMMON MISTAKES

commA–lettER–STRUT: Many accents such as Welsh, West Country and Southern American have a variety of this vowel that has a close to neutral jaw setting. Focus on the drop in the jaw to position 3, and think of the sound as being close to the TRAP vowel.

FOOT–STRUT: Accents of the North of England have no STRUT vowel. They merge these two sets into one using the FOOT vowel for all the STRUT words. Learning the two separate shapes is the first step, but then how do you know which is a FOOT word and which is a STRUT word? This can be tricky as there is no apparent logic in the split! Check on www.howtodoaccents.com and if you're still not sure, ask someone!

NB. The word 'one' is in the STRUT set in Standard English Accents!

4

HOW TO DO...THE FOOT VOWEL SHAPE

Length: **SHORT**

Movement: **STEADY**

Hear It: *Track 26.*

The woman shouldn't put the full pudding onto the butcher's hook.

See It: Illustration + mirror

Feel It:

Jaw: **Position 1, the same position as the KIT vowel.**

Tongue: **The tip of the tongue is relaxed and behind the bottom teeth. The hump in the tongue is at the back and raised.**

Lips/Cheeks: **Cheeks are hollowed, with lips rounded and pushing forward.**

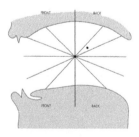

Map/Resonance: **This vowel sits at a mid-back point on the map. The resonance is just behind the midline and has a mid to low quality.**

NOT GOT IT YET?

Hear It: *Track 26 + Funnel.*

Listen again to the whispered vowel shape.

It is important that you can hear the resonant quality of the *shape*, not your voice. If you have the right shape, the resonant note will match the one on the MP3. Bingo!

In order to hear the resonant note of the ***shape*** without the distraction of your voice, whisper the shape with *air only*, and use your funnel. It helps to put a slight 'H' before it.

- Listen to the 'note' that is produced by the ***shape*** as you whisper air through it.

- Compare the note to the one on the MP3 and by subtly changing tongue and lip position, get the notes to match.

- When you are sure that your shape and note match the one on the MP3, add voice to the shape as you breathe out, first on one note, then in your 'spoken' voice.

For other examples of words using this shape go to FOOT in the Kit List sets at www.howtodoaccents.com

COMMON MISTAKES

Flute lips: Flat 'flute lips' (like playing a flute) will kill the low resonance in this sound. Keep the space in the **jaw** between your top and bottom teeth, use a combination of cheek and lip muscles to gently round the **lips** and push them forward from the teeth. You will see the **cheeks** hollowing as you do this.

4

- STRUT–FOOT: Some Northern Irish accents have no FOOT vowel, and use the STRUT shape for all FOOT words. They merge these two sets into one. Learning the two separate shapes is the first step, but then how do you know which is a FOOT word and which is a STRUT word? This can be tricky as there is no apparent logic in the split! Check on www.howtodoaccents.com, and if you're still not sure, ask someone!

- FOOT–GOOSE: Scottish (and some Northern Irish accents) have no FOOT vowel, and use the GOOSE vowel for all FOOT words. Learning the FOOT shape is the first step, but then how do you know which is a FOOT word and which is a GOOSE word? This can be tricky as there is no apparent logic in the split! Check on www.howtodoaccents.com, and if you're still not sure, ask someone!

HOW TO DO...THE GOOSE VOWEL SHAPE

Length: **LONG**

Movement: **STEADY**

Hear It: *Track 27.*

> Two beautiful youths moved through a few smooth, juicy, rude grooves in feudal confusion.

See It: Illustration + mirror

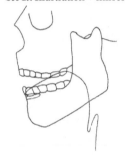

Feel It:

Jaw: **Position 1.**

Tongue: **The tip of the tongue is relaxed and behind the bottom teeth. The hump in the tongue is raised towards the middle of the roof of the mouth.**

Lips/Cheeks: **Cheeks are hollowed, with lips closely rounded and pushing forward.**

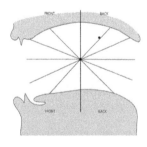

Map/Resonance: **This vowel sits at a high point at the back of the map. The resonance is in the middle and has a mid to low quality.**

NOT GOT IT YET?

Hear It: *Track 27 + Funnel.*

Listen again to the whispered vowel shape.

It is important that you can hear the resonant quality of the ***shape***, not your voice. If you have the right shape, the resonant note will match the one on the MP3. Bingo!

In order to hear the resonant note of the *shape* without the distraction of your voice, whisper the shape with *air only*, and use your funnel. It helps to put a slight 'H' before it.

● Listen to the 'note' that is produced by the *shape* as you whisper air through it.

● Compare the note to the one on the MP3 and by subtly changing tongue and lip position, get the notes to match.

● When you are sure that your shape and note match the one on the MP3, add voice to the shape as you breathe out, first on one note, then in your 'spoken' voice.

For other examples of words using this shape go to GOOSE in the Kit List sets at www.howtodoaccents.com

COMMON MISTAKES

Too far forward and **lack of lip-rounding:** Many contemporary speakers have an extremely unrounded and 'fronted' version of this shape, actually very close to the KIT shape. We recently heard a girl discussing her 'giggle' phone with her friend, only to discover the word she was saying was 'google'! If the hump in the tongue comes forward and the lips unround, the vowel will lose its essential low resonance.

Too far back and 'dark': Old Stage Standard English used a very dark, backed version of this vowel. Although a beautiful sound, nowadays it will give your accent an old-fashioned, dated quality. Be sure to keep the hump of the tongue in the middle of the mouth.

Tongue and lip sliding: Be sure to start the vowel cleanly, rather than sliding into position.

4

TOP TIPS FOR NORTH AMERICANS

This is the shape that often changes to a sliding 'YOO' in some words in Standard English accents. This sliding 'YOO' is a sound you use in your own accents in words such as CUTE and MUSIC. Many North American accents never use this slide after 'D', 'T' and 'N' (e.g. duty = 'dooty', tune = 'toon', new = 'noo') but Standard English Accents do. (See *Environmental Issues*, pages 90-98.)

HOW TO DO...THE FLEECE VOWEL SHAPE

Length: **LONG**

Movement: **STEADY**

Hear It: Track 28.

> The police had reason to believe that Peter, Keith and the anaemic Sheila could be in league to illegally deceive people.

See It: Illustration + mirror

Feel It:

Jaw: **Position 1.**

Tongue: **The hump is forward and high. The hump is aimed at the centre of the gum-ridge.**

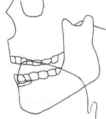

Lips/Cheeks: **Lips a *tiny* bit spread.**

Map/Resonance: **This vowel sits at the front high point of the map. The resonance is at the front and has the highest quality of all.**

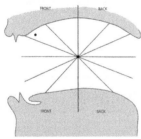

NOT GOT IT YET?

Hear It: Track 28 + Funnel.

Listen again to the whispered vowel shape.

It is important that you can hear the resonant quality of the *shape*, not your voice. If you have the right shape, the resonant note will match the one on the MP3. Bingo!

In order to hear the resonant note of the *shape* without the distraction of your voice, whisper the shape with *air only*, and use your funnel. It helps to put a slight 'H' before it.

- Listen to the 'note' that is produced by the *shape* as you whisper air through it.
- Compare the note to the one on the MP3 and by subtly changing tongue and lip position, get the notes to match.
- When you are sure that your shape and note match the one on the MP3, add voice to the shape as you breathe out, first on one note, then in your 'spoken' voice.

For other examples of words using this shape go to FLEECE in the Kit List sets at www.howtodoaccents.com

COMMON MISTAKES

Lip and cheek tension: Keep the tension focused on the hump in the tongue squeezing high at the front of the mouth while the sides of the tongue are pulled in. The jaw, lips and cheeks remain relaxed. You can check this in a mirror, getting the 'EE' bright without over-spreading the lips. This will ensure that the vowel still has some low overtones to it, in spite of its generally bright quality.

Sliding: As with the GOOSE vowel, there can be a tendency to slide into the 'EE'. Be sure to lift the tongue into position immediately.

Dull or not bright enough: Aim the hump to the centre point of the gumridge, not too far forward (rolling out of the mouth) nor too flat or soft. Keep it tight.

4

TOP TIPS FOR NORTH AMERICANS

North Americans are likely to make just the same mistakes as Brits, so read the notes above!

HOW TO DO...THE NURSE VOWEL SHAPE

Length: **LONG**

Movement: **STEADY**

Hear It: Track 29.

Pearl urged Myrtle's attorney to rehearse a certain circus turn before the courteous worm turned.

See It: Illustration + mirror

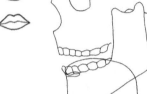

Feel It:

Jaw: **Position 1 (neutral).**

Tongue: **Neutral and relaxed (the hump will sit in the centre of the mouth).**

Lips/Cheeks: **Neutral and relaxed.**

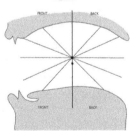

Map/Resonance: This vowel sits in the midpoint of the map. The resonance is in the middle of the mouth and has a mid-note quality.

NOT GOT IT YET?

Hear It: Track 29 + Funnel.

Listen again to the whispered vowel shape.

It is important that you can hear the resonant quality of the *shape*, not your voice. If you have the right shape, the resonant note will match the one on the MP3. Bingo!

In order to hear the resonant note of the *shape* without the distraction of your voice, whisper the shape with *air only*, and use your funnel. It helps to put a slight 'H' before it.

● Listen to the 'note' that is produced by the *shape* as you whisper air through it.

● Compare the note to the one on the MP3 and by subtly changing tongue and lip position, get the notes to match.

● When you are sure that your shape and note match the one on the MP3, add voice to the shape as you breathe out, first on one note, then in your 'spoken' voice.

For other examples of words using this shape go to NURSE in the Kit List sets at www.howtodoaccents.com

COMMON MISTAKES

The lips and tongue are absolutely RELAXED in this shape. There should be no bending, rounding or spreading at all. Look in the mirror to check your lip shape with this one, don't trust your ear!

'R' bend: See *Top Tips for North Americans.*

Lip-rounding: See *Top Tips for North Americans.*

Too open: If the jaw drops open too far the vowel will sound too upper class, and not neutral.

Too far forward: If the tongue rolls forward from the midpoint the vowel will have an 'E' quality. Great for Liverpool, but not for a New Standard English Accent!

4

TOP TIPS FOR NORTH AMERICANS

'R' bend: In spite of the fact that there is always an 'R' in the spelling, there is *no 'R' and nothing like an 'R'*, in this vowel shape. It is a long *steady* vowel. If you follow the instructions for the commA vowel (see pages 95-96) and then lengthen it, you will be making the Neutral Standard English Accent NURSE vowel.

It can really help to rewrite the words without the 'R' in them, like this:

Nurse = 'Nuhss'   Pearl = 'Puhl'   World = 'Wuhld', etc.

Lip-rounding: Once you have got rid of the 'R', the next foible is lip-rounding. Any contraction of the lips will give this a 'mid-Atlantic' quality, like the old movie stars, or a Welsh quality. For a New Standard English Accent, keep the lips completely relaxed. Practise this one in the mirror!

HOW TO DO...THE TRAP VOWEL SHAPE

Length: **SHORT**

Movement: **STEADY**

Hear It: *Track 30.*

> The cat dashed to catch the ham that dangled from the bag.

See It: Illustration + mirror

Feel It:

Jaw: **Position 3.**

Tongue: **The hump is slightly forward, the body of the tongue relaxed.**

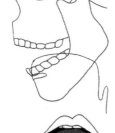

Lips/Cheeks: **Open and Relaxed with a little spread in the corners.**

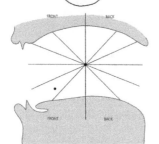

Map/Resonance: **This vowel sits at the front/ low point on the map. The resonance is at the front and has a midnote quality, between 'UH' and 'E'.**

NOT GOT IT YET?

Hear It: *Track 30 + Funnel.*

Listen again to the whispered vowel shape.

It is important that you can hear the resonant quality of the *shape*, not your voice. If you have the right shape, the resonant note will match the one on the MP3. Bingo!

In order to hear the resonant note of the *shape* without the distraction of your voice, whisper the shape with *air only*, and use your funnel. It helps to put a slight 'H' before it.

● Listen to the 'note' that is produced by the *shape* as you whisper air through it.

● Compare the note to the one on the MP3 and by subtly changing tongue and lip position, get the notes to match.

● When you are sure that your shape and note match the one on the MP3, add voice to the shape as you breathe out, first on one note, then in your 'spoken' voice.

For other examples of words using this shape go to TRAP in the Kit List sets at www.howtodoaccents.com

NB. Trans and 'astic' words: There is a little subset of words that tend to jump between the TRAP and BATH sets in Standard English Accents. Here are some examples...

Transport   Transfer   Transient   Plastic   Elastic   Drastic

The 'astic' words have firmly moved into the TRAP set in a New Standard English Accent. Try saying them as BATH words with an 'AH' and you'll hear how old-fashioned, and even comical they now sound!

The Trans words, however, are still very fluid. Many New Standard English Accent speakers will treat some as BATH words with a long 'AH' and some as TRAP words, with a short 'A'. We suspect that they are moving the same way as the 'astic' words but only time will tell!

COMMON MISTAKES

This vowel can present quite a hurdle for some. Too far back and it will be a Northern Vowel, too far forward and raised towards 'E' and it will sound very Wartime Wendies and BBC Berties. If the soft palate is low the sound will disappear down the nose, and if the back of the tongue is tense it can give it a harsh quality! It is seriously affected by the Foundations, so be sure to check those before you begin work on this vowel.

Too far back/tense: First release the back of the tongue by stretching the tongue out of the mouth, as far as it will go, and then letting it slide back in on its own. Then, with the tongue tip anchored behind your bottom teeth, roll the front of the tongue forward while letting the jaw drop open. The jaw drops open completely creating maximum space, without tension.

Too raised: There should be no hint of the DRESS vowel in this shape, or your accent will sound 50 years out of date!

Nasalised: While that tongue rolls forward, open the space behind it by lifting the soft palate a little.

4

TOP TIPS FOR NORTH AMERICANS

HAT–HAND (nasalisation): In most North American accents you can hear a difference between the vowel in HAT and the vowel in HAND (see page 91).

Marry–Merry ('R' colouring): In most North American accents this vowel is also strongly affected by 'R' colouring, again leading to the vowel being raised towards an 'E' (see page 93).

HOW TO DO...THE BATH–PALM–START VOWEL

Length: **LONG**

Movement: **STEADY**

Hear It: Track 31.

BATH: 'Francis the calf can't dance,' laughed Sandra the giraffe, aghast, as the calf pranced disastrously.

PALM: Brahms' sonata kept father calm in the spa.'

START: Sergeant Charles was the star of the party with his hearty aria.

See It: Illustration + mirror

Feel It:

Jaw: **Position 3.**

Tongue: **The tip of the tongue is relaxed and behind the bottom teeth. There is a slight hump in the back of the tongue.**

Lips/Cheeks: **Neutral and relaxed.**

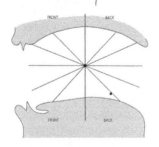

Map/Resonance: **The vowel sits at the low back point of the map. The resonance is at the back and has a mid-note quality.**

NOT GOT IT YET?

Hear It: Track 31 + Funnel.

Listen again to the whispered vowel shape.

It is important that you can hear the resonant quality of the *shape*, not your voice. If you have the right shape, the resonant note will match the one on the MP3. Bingo!

In order to hear the resonant note of the **shape** without the distraction of your voice, whisper the shape with *air only*, and use your funnel. It helps to put a slight 'H' before it.

● Listen to the 'note' that is produced by the **shape** as you whisper air through it.

● Compare the note to the one on the MP3 and by subtly changing tongue and lip position, get the notes to match.

● When you are sure that your shape and note match the one on the MP3, add voice to the shape as you breathe out, first on one note, then in your 'spoken' voice.

For other examples of words using this shape go to BATH-PALM-START in the Kit List sets at www.howtodoaccents.com

COMMON MISTAKES

Not fully merging: One of the trickiest things is that what may be two or three shapes in your own accent are merged to just one in Standard English Accents. The vowels in these sets must sound *identical!* Here are a couple of sentences to help test yourself:

Francis's Father is a disaster in a car. He can't keep calm for a start.

BATH–TRAP merging: Many accents, including those of North America and the North of England, merge BATH words with TRAP words. These sets are *separate* so you will need to know which words belong in the BATH set and which in the TRAP set. This is notoriously difficult to determine. There are rules, but there will always be the odd word that doesn't follow the rules. Here are some initial guidelines: *Single syllable words with 'TH', 'F' or 'S' after the 'A' (bath, pass, last, daft, etc.). Two syllables ending 'ER' (after, laughter), and most 'NT' 'ND' 'NS' and 'NCH' words (plant, demand, dance, branch) all have an 'AH' vowel.* There are others. For more check BATH in the Kit List sets at www.howtodoaccents.com. If you are still not sure, ask someone!

PALM inconsistencies: This set has many oddities in it. In Standard English Accents all PALM words, whether they are spelled with an 'L' or not, have no 'L' in the pronunciation. They just have the 'AH' vowel shape.

See www.howtodoaccents.com for more words in the PALM Set.

4

TOP TIPS FOR NORTH AMERICANS

Not Fully Merging: These sets must sound *identical!* (see above).
BATH–TRAP Merged: They need separating! (see above).
Back of tongue gripping + lip-rounding: This vowel should not be too 'dark' in quality. Think 'AH' as you drop the jaw completely, keep the tip of the tongue behind the bottom teeth, and relax the back and the lips. This is especially important with PALM words, including the word FATHER. PALM, CALM, FATHER and ASK are common words in scripts. Mark them up and practise them using the 'AH' vowel shape.

TOP TIP

The words CAN'T and AFTER are two that are extremely frequent and really worth marking in any script you are working on. In our experience they are the ones that most commonly go astray.

HOW TO DO...THE LOT–CLOTH VOWEL SHAPE

Length: **SHORT**

Movement: **STEADY**

Hear It: Track 32.

> **LOT:** Tom honestly acknowledged how top-notch the swan was to dodge the yacht.
>
> **CLOTH:** Ross often frothed the coffee and washed the long sausages in Boston.

See It: Illustration + mirror

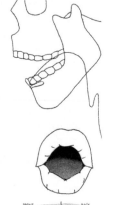

Feel It:

Jaw: **Position 3.**

Tongue: **The tip of the tongue is relaxed and behind the bottom teeth. There is a slight hump in the back of the tongue.**

Lips/Cheeks: **Cheeks are hollowed, with lips gently rounded, pushing gently forward.**

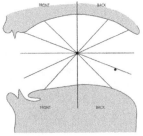

Map/Resonance: **This vowel sits towards the low back point on the map. The resonance is at the back of the mouth and has a low quality.**

NOT GOT IT YET?

Hear It: Track 32 + Funnel.

Listen again to the whispered vowel shape.

It is important that you can hear the resonant quality of the *shape*, not your voice. If you have the right shape, the resonant note will match the one on the MP3. Bingo!

How To Do Standard English Accents

In order to hear the resonant note of the **shape** without the distraction of your voice, whisper the shape with *air only*, and use your funnel. It helps to put a slight 'H' before it.

- Listen to the 'note' that is produced by the **shape** as you whisper air through it.

- Compare the note to the one on the MP3 and by subtly changing tongue and lip position, get the notes to match.

- When you are sure that your shape and note match the one on the MP3, add voice to the shape as you breathe out, first on one note, then in your 'spoken' voice.

For other examples of words using this shape go to LOT-CLOTH in the Kit List sets at www.howtodoaccents.com

COMMON MISTAKES

Lack of lip-rounding: 'Promote' the lips by pushing them slightly forward away from the teeth while also rounding them. This extends the length of the oral cavity. It is this added length, together with the rounded opening, that brings low resonance into the sound that is so important for the richness of the New Standard English sound!

4

TOP TIPS FOR NORTH AMERICANS

Lack of lip-rounding: Practise having a fully open jaw while also rounding the lips. This can be an unusual feeling for North American mouths!

LOT–THOUGHT merging: Many contemporary North American accents have one shape for these two sets. Remember the LOT set is open, round and SHORT!

BATH–LOT–THOUGHT: Work on finding these three English stop off points for the back of the tongue. They are pretty close together, and in a place where many North Americans have only one shape to worry about! As they are so close together, it is the length, as much as the shape that counts! Remember:

BATH = long, jaw 3, lips neutral

LOT = short, jaw 3, lips round

THOUGHT = long, jaw 2, lips round

NB. Learning to distinguish the LOT set from the THOUGHT set is not just useful for English accents, but also for many East Coast and Southern American accents too!

HOW TO DO...THE THOUGHT–NORTH–FORCE (TOUR) VOWEL SHAPE

Length: **LONG**

Movement: **STEADY**

Hear It: Track 33.

THOUGHT: Paul applauded all the naughty daughters who yawned when taught with chalk and talk.

NORTH: George cavorted with Thor to fortify his short torso for the war in York.

FORCE: 'Of course I adore Nora', roared the porter through the door to the four divorced boarders.

(**TOUR:** Muriel assured the poor tourists that the insurance was sure to cover Europe.) *See note on page 75.*

See It: Illustration + mirror

 Feel It:

Jaw: **Position 2.**

Tongue: **The tip of the tongue is relaxed and behind the bottom teeth. The hump is at the back of the tongue and raised a little higher than LOT–CLOTH.**

Lips/Cheeks: **Cheeks are hollowed, with lips gently rounded and pushing forward.**

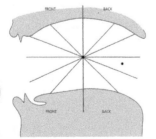

Map/Resonance: **This vowel sits close to the midline at the back of the map. The resonance is at the back and has a low quality.**

NOT GOT IT YET?

Hear It: Track 33 + Funnel.

Listen again to the whispered vowel shape.

It is important that you can hear the resonant quality of the *shape*, not your voice. If you have the right shape, the resonant note will match the one on the MP3. Bingo!

In order to hear the resonant note of the *shape* without the distraction of your voice, whisper the shape with *air only*, and use your funnel. It helps to put a slight 'H' before it.

- Listen to the 'note' that is produced by the *shape* as you whisper air through it.
- Compare the note to the one on the MP3 and by subtly changing tongue and lip position, get the notes to match.
- When you are sure that your shape and note match the one on the MP3, add voice to the shape as you breathe out, first on one note, then in your 'spoken' voice.

For other examples of words using this shape go to THOUGHT-NORTH-FORCE (TOUR) in the Kit List sets at www.howtodoaccents.com

COMMON MISTAKES

Jaw and Lips too open: Keeping the jaw in position 2, use cheek and lip muscles to gently round the lips and push them forward. You will see the cheeks hollowing. You will see that the open circle created by the lips is smaller than the LOT–CLOTH opening, about the size of a thumb.

Lips too tight: Though the lips are rounded they are not tight. The cheeks push the lips forward.

4

TOP TIPS FOR NORTH AMERICANS

LOT–THOUGHT distinction: It is essential to separate these sets in order to do NSEA. One of the biggest challenges is learning to identify the THOUGHT words. Look for these spellings:

OUGH (ought) AUGH (taught) AU (Paul) AL (walk) AW (saw)

Then make the shape *identical* to the NORTH set! When a New Standard English speaker says the words SAW and SORE you would not be able to hear which word was which. They are phonetically identical. Here are some more identical pairs to practise:

CAUGHT–COURT LAW–LORE PAW–POUR FLAW–FLOOR

NB. **TOUR.** After some deliberation we decided to include the TOUR set in this merger, though this is not necessarily the case for all TOUR words. Standard English Accents *used* to have a sliding vowel for this set, sliding from the FOOT vowel to the schwa, /ʊə/, but this slide has all but disappeared from contemporary standard speech. In its place you will now hear the THOUGHT vowel in some words, such as POOR, and the NURSE VOWEL or a new long vowel similar to a FOOT shape in words such as JURY and EUROPE.

HOW TO DO...THE FACE VOWEL SHAPE

Length: **LONG**

Movement: **SLIDING**

Hear It: Track 34.

> April felt faint as she campaigned to rein in the wasteful ladies to change their ways and obey.

See It: Illustration + mirror

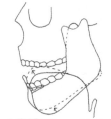

Feel It:

Jaw: **Position slides from 2 to 1.**

Tongue: The tip of the tongue is relaxed and behind the bottom teeth. The hump in the tongue slides from the DRESS shape to between the KIT and FLEECE shapes.

Lips/Cheeks: **Neutral.**

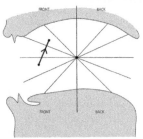

Map/Resonance: The vowel is at the front of the map. The resonance is at the front and has a fairly high quality.

NOT GOT IT YET?

Hear It: Track 34 + Funnel.

Listen again to the whispered vowel shape.

It is important that you can hear the resonant quality of the *shape*, not your voice. If you have the right shape, the resonant note will match the one on the MP3. Bingo!

In order to hear the resonant note of the *shape* without the distraction of your voice, whisper the shape with *air only*, and use your funnel. It helps to put a slight 'H' before it.

- Listen to the 'note' that is produced by the *shape* as you whisper air through it.
- Compare the note to the one on the MP3 and by subtly changing tongue and lip position, get the notes to match.
- When you are sure that your shape and note match the one on the MP3, add voice to the shape as you breathe out, first on one note, then in your 'spoken' voice.

For other examples of words using this shape go to FACE in the Kit List sets at www.howtodoaccents.com

COMMON MISTAKES

Starting too open/back: It is so important to start this slide from the standard DRESS position. Check the DRESS page for extra help. If the start shape begins to drift towards TRAP, even slightly, it will not sound neutral.

Closing to 'EE': Squeezing into a tight 'EE' will not sound neutral. Be sure to place the 'weight' in the first half of the slide lightly to KIT.

Too small a slide: If the start position is too raised the slide will not be big enough, giving it almost a monophthong quality as is heard in Scottish accents. This can give the accent an old-fashioned or upper-class quality.

4

TOP TIPS FOR NORTH AMERICANS

North Americans are likely to make just the same mistakes as Brits, so see the notes above!

HOW TO DO...THE GOAT VOWEL SHAPE
(...and the **GOAL** vowel shape...)

Length: **LONG**

Movement: **SLIDING**

Hear It: *Track 35.*

> Joan coaxed her beau, Owen to grow bolder, though she loathed over-controlling soldiers.

Goat–Goal. The New Standard English Accent has two distinct versions of this vowel. This is as a result of the L Effect (see page 94). Whenever this vowel is followed by a dark 'L' (bolder soldier) it changes its starting shape from the commA vowel or schwa (see page 96) to the LOT vowel. This will also happen on words that are *built* from words with a dark 'L', e.g. Goal–Goalie Control–Controlling.

See It: Illustration + mirror

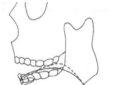

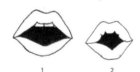

1   2

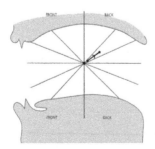

Feel It:

Jaw: **Position 1.**
L Effect: Slides from Position 2 to 1.
Tongue: **The tip of the tongue is relaxed and behind the bottom teeth. The hump in the tongue starts in neutral and slides a small distance to the FOOT shape.**
L Effect: The hump starts in the LOT shape and slides to FOOT.

Lips/Cheeks: **Start with a slight amount of rounding in preparation for the small slide to the FOOT vowel shape.**
L Effect: Start rounded in LOT position and slide to FOOT.

Map/Resonance: **The vowel begins in the midpoint of the map and slides to the back. The resonance moves from a mid to low quality.**
L Effect: The vowel is at the back of the map, with a small closing slide. The resonance has a low quality.

NOT GOT IT YET?

Hear It: Track 35 + Funnel.

Listen again to the whispered vowel shape.

Remember, it is important that you can hear the resonant note of the *shape*, not your voice. If you have the right shape, the resonant note will match the one on the MP3. Bingo!

In order to hear the resonant note of the *shape* without the distraction of your voice, whisper through the shape with *air only*.

● Listen to the 'note' that is produced by the *shape* as you whisper air through it.

● Compare the note to the one on the MP3.

● By subtly changing tongue position, get the notes to match.

● When you are sure that your shape and note match the one on the MP3, add voice to the shape as you breathe out, first on one note, then in your 'spoken' voice.

For other examples of words using this shape go to GOAT in the Kit List sets at www.howtodoaccents.com

COMMON MISTAKES

Not distinguishing **GOAT** and *GOAL*.

Older varieties of Standard English have the same sound for GOAT and GOAL. It is a major contributor to their old-fashioned quality.

Does your accent keep them the same? If so, you may need extra practice to separate them if you don't want that old-fashioned sound.

The **o**ver-contr**oll**ing s**o**ldier was wearing a br**o**ken b**owl**er hat, an **o**ld m**o**hair c**oat**, and was sm**o**king from a long g**o**lden cigarette-h**o**lder.

M**o**toring along in her Sk**o**da, h**o**lding a fur st**o**le **o**ver her sh**ou**lder, the p**o**le-dancer h**o**ped not to pay the t**o**ll for the br**o**ken r**oa**d.

Too open: The GOAT shape is a small slide. It must start from the neutral schwa position (see page 96). Too far forward and it will sound more upper class, too open and it will sound more London or West Midlands. You will feel the movement mostly in the lips. Put your little finger between your lips and then round your lips around it: this is the movement of the lips during the GOAT vowel.

HOW TO DO...THE PRICE VOWEL SHAPE

Length: **LONG**

Movement: **SLIDING.** The weight is longer and heavier in the first half of the sound, shorter and lighter in the second half.

Hear It: *Track 36.*

> Friday is the right night to arrive by bicycle in Cyprus to buy a fine eiderdown.

See It: Illustration + mirror

Feel It:

Jaw: **Position slides from 3 to 1.**

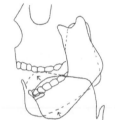

Tongue: **The tip of the tongue is relaxed and behind the bottom teeth. The hump in the tongue slides from halfway between the TRAP and STRUT shape to a relaxed FLEECE shape.**

Lips/Cheeks: **Slide from the TRAP shape to the FLEECE shape.**

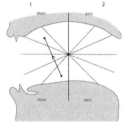

Map/Resonance: **The vowel slides from the middle to the front of the map. The resonance moves from the middle to the front, going from a mid to a high quality.**

NOT GOT IT YET?

Hear It: *Track 36 + Funnel.*

Listen again to the whispered vowel shape.

It is important that you can hear the resonant quality of the *shape*, not your voice. If you have the right shape, the resonant note will match the one on the MP3. Bingo!

In order to hear the resonant note of the *shape* without the distraction of your voice, whisper the shape with *air only*, and use your funnel. It helps to put a slight 'H' before it.

- Listen to the 'note' that is produced by the *shape* as you whisper air through it.

- Compare the note to the one on the MP3 and by subtly changing tongue and lip position, get the notes to match.

- When you are sure that your shape and note match the one on the MP3, add voice to the shape as you breathe out, first on one note, then in your 'spoken' voice.

For other examples of words using this shape go to PRICE in the Kit List sets at www.howtodoaccents.com

COMMON MISTAKES

This is the vowel used for the personal pronoun 'I'. As such it seems to be closely connected to identity and is really susceptible to migrating back to your own accent, especially in heightened emotional scenes. Here are some of the main issues to watch for:

Nasality: Get that soft palate up and let the vowel come forward. Keep the tongue tip touching the back of your lower front teeth and think of a yawning as you make this shape.

Starting from a commA vowel: Many accents of the West of England start from a commA vowel. Be sure to drop the jaw open beyond neutral and perhaps favour the TRAP vowel as you start the slide.

Starting from the BATH–START shape: If the slide starts too far back the accent will have a London quality. If this is what your accent does, favour the TRAP vowel as your starting position.

Squeezing to 'EE': Tightening to 'EE' gives the accent a strong regional quality. Put the weight into the first half of the slide and slide very gently to a soft FLEECE shape.

TOP TIPS FOR NORTH AMERICANS

Some North American accents, such as Canadian accents, use a much tighter slide when the sound following it is voiceless. Compare the vowel shapes you use in the following:

buy–bide–bike   rye–ride–right

In a New Standard English Accent the shape is the same in all three words!

HOW TO DO...THE CHOICE VOWEL SHAPE

Length: **LONG**

Movement: **SLIDING.** The weight is longer and heavier in the first half of the sound, shorter and lighter in the second half.

Hear It: Track 37.

> The boy employed a joist to hoist the moist oysters into the boiling oil.

See It: Illustration + mirror

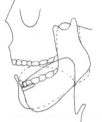

Feel It:

Jaw: **Position slides from 2 to 1.**

Tongue: **The tip of the tongue is relaxed and behind the bottom teeth. The hump in the tongue slides from the THOUGHT shape to a relaxed FLEECE shape.**

Lips/Cheeks: **Slide very gently from the THOUGHT shape to a relaxed FLEECE shape.**

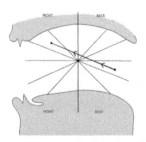

Map/Resonance: **The vowel slides from the back to the front of the map. The resonance moves from the back to the front and from a low to a high quality.**

NOT GOT IT YET?

Hear It: Track 37 + Funnel.

Listen again to the whispered vowel shape.

It is important that you can hear the resonant quality of the *shape*, not your voice. If you have the right shape, the resonant note will match the one on the MP3. Bingo!

In order to hear the resonant note of the *shape* without the distraction of your voice, whisper the shape with *air only*, and use your funnel. It helps to put a slight 'H' before it.

- Listen to the 'note' that is produced by the *shape* as you whisper air through it.
- Compare the note to the one on the MP3 and by subtly changing tongue and lip position, get the notes to match.
- When you are sure that your shape and note match the one on the MP3, add voice to the shape as you breathe out, first on one note, then in your 'spoken' voice.

For other examples of words using this shape go to CHOICE in the Kit List sets at www.howtodoaccents.com

COMMON MISTAKES

As the biggest slide in this accent, the only issue is a tendency to give it too much muscle and spring.

Tongue: Put the weight in the first half and *glide* to a soft FLEECE shape.

Lips: Keep them soft and relaxed throughout.

4

HOW TO DO...THE MOUTH VOWEL SHAPE

Length: **LONG**

Movement: **SLIDING.** The weight and length are on the first half of the sound, with the second half lighter and shorter.

Hear It: *Track 38.*

> The loud crowd from south of the county wanted to oust the clown out of town, but they were all mouth.

See It: Illustration + mirror

Feel It:

Jaw: **Slides from position 3 to 1.**

Tongue: **The tip of the tongue is relaxed and behind the bottom teeth. The hump in the tongue slides from halfway between the TRAP and STRUT shape to the FOOT shape.**

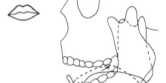

Lips/Cheeks: **Start in TRAP shape and round to the FOOT shape.**

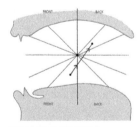

Map/Resonance: **The vowel begins in the low midpoint of the map and slides up and back. The resonance moves from the middle to the back of the mouth and from mid to low.**

NOT GOT IT YET?

Hear It: *Track 38 + Funnel.*

Listen again to the whispered vowel shape.

It is important that you can hear the resonant note of the ***shape***, not your voice. If you have the right shape, the resonant note will match the one on the MP3. Bingo!

In order to hear the resonant note of the *shape* without the distraction of your voice, whisper through the shape with *air only*.

- Listen to the 'note' that is produced by the *shape* as you whisper air through it.
- Compare the note to the one on the MP3.
- By subtly changing tongue position, get the notes to match.
- Listen to Jan 'tune in' her shape to match Edda's.
- When you are sure that your shape and note match the one on the MP3, add voice to the shape as you breathe out, first on one note, then in your 'spoken' voice.

For other examples of words using this shape go to MOUTH in the Kit List sets at www.howtodoaccents.com

COMMON MISTAKES

Nasality: Keep a slight sense of yawn in the back of the mouth to keep the soft palate up and prevent nasal spill (see pages 92-93).

Tongue tension: Relax the back of the tongue, keep the tip forward.

4

TOP TIPS FOR NORTH AMERICANS

Canadian and older Virginian accents use a tighter shape when the next sound is a voiceless consonant. Compare the vowel shapes you use in the following:

POW–POUT   HOW–HOUSE   LOUD–LOUT

In New Standard English Accents the shape from the first word is kept in the second.

HOW TO DO...THE NEAR VOWEL SHAPE

Length: **LONG**

Movement: **SLIDING.** The weight is longer and heavier in the first half of the sound, shorter and lighter in the second half.

Hear It: *Track 39.*

> Maria was sincere in her weird career, but feared the fierce bearded cashier.

See It: Illustration + mirror

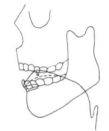

Feel It:

Jaw: **Position 1.**

Tongue: **The tip of the tongue is relaxed and behind the bottom teeth. The hump in the tongue slides from the KIT shape, high at the front of the mouth, to neutral.**

Lips/Cheeks: **Start in the KIT shape and relax to neutral.**

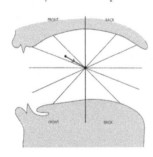

Map/Resonance: **The vowel slides from the front of the map to the midpoint. The resonance moves from the front to the middle of the mouth and from a high to mid-note quality.**

NOT GOT IT YET?

Hear It: *Track 39 + Funnel.*

Listen again to the whispered vowel shape.

It is important that you can hear the resonant quality of the *shape*, not your voice. If you have the right shape, the resonant note will match the one on the MP3. Bingo!

In order to hear the resonant note of the *shape* without the distraction of your voice, whisper the shape with *air only*, and use your funnel. It helps to put a slight 'H' before it.

● Listen to the 'note' that is produced by the *shape* as you whisper air through it.

● Compare the note to the one on the MP3 and by subtly changing tongue and lip position, get the notes to match.

● When you are sure that your shape and note match the one on the MP3, add voice to the shape as you breathe out, first on one note, then in your 'spoken' voice.

For other examples of words using this shape go to NEAR in the Kit List sets at www.howtodoaccents.com

COMMON MISTAKES

Keeping it steady: Some regional accents hold the jaw and tongue in a long KIT shape. Be sure to relax the tongue and the jaw back to the neutral commA vowel or schwa.

Bouncing 'ee-yu': This is a very gentle slide. *Relax* the tongue back to neutral.

4

TOP TIPS FOR NORTH AMERICANS

'R': There is no 'R' in this slide! Drop the 'R' and replace it with a commA vowel or schwa. However, if the next word starts with a vowel, the 'R' will come back, *very lightly*, to start the next word!

near = 'neeuh'   near and far = 'neeuh rand fah'

For more on this feature see *Planet Non-Rhotic*, pages 43-48.

HOW TO DO...THE SQUARE VOWEL SHAPE

Length: **LONG**

Movement: **STEADY or GENTLY SLIDING**

Hear It: Track 40.

Where the pears are scarce, the bears share theirs fairly.

See It: Illustration + mirror

Feel It:

Jaw: **Position 2 with a possible slide to 1 (neutral).**

Tongue: **The tip of the tongue is relaxed and behind the bottom teeth. The hump in the tongue sits in the DRESS vowel position, at the front of the mouth, with a possible slide to neutral.**

Lips/Cheeks: **Start in the DRESS shape and relax to neutral.**

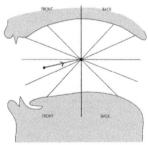

Map/Resonance: **The vowel is at the front of the map with a possible slide to the midpoint. The resonance is at the front and has a mid-note quality.**

NOT GOT IT YET?

Hear It: Track 40 + Funnel.

Listen again to the whispered vowel shape.

It is important that you can hear the resonant quality of the *shape*, not your voice. If you have the right shape, the resonant note will match the one on the MP3. Bingo!

In order to hear the resonant note of the **shape** without the distraction of your voice, whisper the shape with *air only*, and use your funnel. It helps to put a slight 'H' before it.

● Listen to the 'note' that is produced by the **shape** as you whisper air through it.

● Compare the note to the one on the MP3 and by subtly changing tongue and lip position, get the notes to match.

● When you are sure that your shape and note match the one on the MP3, add voice to the shape as you breathe out, first on one note, then in your 'spoken' voice.

For other examples of words using this shape go to SQUARE in the Kit List sets at www.howtodoaccents.com

COMMON MISTAKES

This vowel has changed over time and is now caught between being a sliding and a steady vowel. It would seem that the steady version is on the increase and is more contemporary neutral than the slide, which sounds a little old-fashioned or upper class.

If you use the steady vowel it is essential to have the right Foundations, with the tongue released into a gentle DRESS position, not too tense and not too open.

TOP TIPS FOR NORTH AMERICANS

'R': There is no 'R' in this slide! Drop the 'R' and replace it with a commA vowel or schwa (see page 96), or hold the tongue steady behind the bottom teeth. However, if the next word starts with a vowel, the 'R' will come back, *very lightly*, to start the next word!

square = 'skwe-uh' square and round = 'skwe rand rownd'

For more on this feature see *Planet Non-Rhotic*, pages 43-48.

ENVIRONMENTAL ISSUES

Through using the Kit List you can gather the fundamental information you need on the shapes the accent uses, and the way the vowels are distributed. Those are the basic essentials. But a vowel is a little like a person; change the environment and you might change the way it behaves. Wouldn't you behave differently surrounded by palm trees from when you're surrounded by concrete? Vowels are the same. They often behave very differently depending on whether they stand alone or cluster together, which consonants follow them, and whether they are stressed or not.

Vowel Clusters and Collisions

The Neutral Standard English Accent **GLIDES** through clusters and collisions.

Hear It: Track 41.

Listen to these example words:

> tower   higher   going   lying

When two vowels from the Kit List meet, new slides are created, sometimes sliding through three or more shapes. For example in the word 'created', the FLEECE vowel meets the FACE vowel, making an 'EEAY' slide.

> CREE–AYTED

This can also happen when a word ending is added such as 'ING' and 'ER'...

> GO–ING   PLAY–ER

and when words meet...

> GO OUT   DO IT   PLAY ON

Hear It: Track 42.

The question is, how do you handle the clusters and collisions? Are you:

- **Gliding**: Moving quickly and clearly through each of the vowel shapes ('sa–i–uh–nce'):
  > tah–oo–uh   ha–i–uh   gu–oo–ing   la–i–ing

- **Inserting**: Adding a springing consonant, 'W', 'R', or 'Y', making a new syllable:
  to bounce into (science = 'sci–Yence'):
  > ta–wuh   ha–yuh   go–wing   ly–ying

- **Smoothing**: Ironing out the slide, partially or completely (science = 'sahnce'):
  > taah   haah   geng   lahing

'ER' and 'ING' endings make some of the most obvious clusters, so if you are a bouncer or a smoother, first practise gliding with these, and then try the paragraph below.

Hear It: Track 43.

+ 'ER'

NB. As a Non-Rhotic accent these become clusters of a sliding vowel + SCHWA

PLAYER (FACE vowel + 'UH')

LAWYER (CHOICE vowel + 'UH')

MOWER (GOAT vowel + 'UH')

HIGHER (PRICE vowel + 'UH')

TOWER (MOUTH vowel + 'UH')

+ 'ING'

FLEEING (FLEECE vowel + 'ING')

CHEWING (GOOSE vowel + 'ING')

PLAYING (FACE vowel + 'ING')

GOING (GOAT vowel + 'ING')

PLOUGHING (MOUTH vowel + 'ING')

LYING (PRICE vowel + 'ING')

ANNOYING (CHOICE vowel + 'ING')

Hear It: Track 44 and *Feel It:* Listen to our speaker gliding through the vowel collisions in this paragraph and then have a go yourself.

We were **going to a** party in **Lower** Loxeley, bowling along with considerable **power, trying** to get **to it** on time. '**Who are** we **seeing** there?' I asked. 'Oh, some very **annoying** people', he answered. 'There'll be **Howard**, the incessant card **player**, and **my Aunt** the **lawyer, doing** her usual party piece. They'll be in the **drawing** room, gathered around the fire, **chewing** the fat, **playing** "who is the smartest" **allowing** no one else to get a word in. How **tiresome!**'

Nasal Colouring and Spilling

There is **NO nasal colouring or spilling** in a New Standard English Accent.

Sounds revolting, but to make an 'N', 'M' or 'NG' the soft palate drops down, opening the passage to the nose and sending the sound into the nasal cavity.

In *some* accents the soft palate drops *before* the 'N', 'M' or 'NG', sending the *vowel* down the nose too. That is what we call nasal colouring. If the soft palate is *permanently* low, that creates nasal spill.

TOP TIPS FOR NORTH AMERICANS

Nasal colouring and spilling affect the Foundations, and vice versa. It is a strong feature of many North American accents. Cleaning it up may take a bit of focus, but it will ensure that your Foundations are solid.

Hear It: Track 45. Listen to the following list of word pairs.

Feel It: Have a go yourself, keeping the vowel in the second word clean of nasal colouring. Keep that soft palate up until the 'N', 'M' or 'NG', and get the two vowels to sound exactly the same!

bit v bin	daft v dance	swore v sworn
head v hen	bra v Brahms	fate v fame
but v bun	bark v barn	moat v moan
loop v loom	cot v con	pride v prime
feet v fiend	soft v song	joy v join
first v firm	taught v taunt	pout v pound
bad v band	fork v form	career v Korean

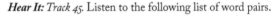

Hear It and *Feel It: Track 46.* If you're ready for the challenge, try this paragraph. We've marked the pairs in bold. Be sure to get the vowel in the following pairs to sound the same. Keep them out of your nose!

Beth and **Glen** went to the **mad man's daft dance** party. They were **kitted** in **bin** liners, **just** for **fun**. At the sound of a **blues tune**, Glen's **feet** moved **fiendishly** but Beth preferred to **purr** and **squirm** to **Bach** and **Brahms**. As the **bad band** played, the dogs **barked** in the **barn**. The evening went on and a **lot** of **honest soft songs** were sung. Glen **taught** the boys to **taunt** the girls with their **corking forms**. By midnight he **swore** he was **worn** out. Let's **face** it, **fame** is tiring. He got his **coat** and **moaned**, 'I suffer from **pride**, but I'm past my **prime**. It was a **joy** to **join** in. I **pouted** and **pounded** my feet, but now I must resume my **career** teaching **Korean** to **Blair's bairns**.'

'R' Colouring

There is **NO 'R'** Colouring in a NSEA.

In all Standard English Accents, vowels and 'Rs' are clearly separated, so 'R' Colouring simply doesn't happen. In some Rhotic accents, however, vowels can get *seriously* affected when there's an 'R' coming up. As the tongue prepares to shape 'R', the vowel gets pulled with it, and you hear the 'R' 'sitting' on the vowel.

Hear It: Track 47. Listen to this pair of words, first with heavy 'R' Colouring, then mild, then none:

> Cat–Carry

Because all Standard English Accents are *Non*-Rhotic, they only use the 'R' to *start* syllables. The 'R' is used to bounce into the next vowel, not sit on the last one! Nowhere is this more noticeable than when the 'R' is slap bang in the middle of a word.

4

TOP TIPS FOR NORTH AMERICANS

If you have an accent that uses 'R' Colouring it can *seriously* corrupt your Standard English Accents. Go though the following list of words, saying the first syllable on its own, then the second, then say the word again using the new, light, mid-word bounce.

HU–REE hurry	STAH–REE starry
MI–RUH mirror	SO–REE sorry
TE–RUH terror	BO–ROH borrow
HA–REE harry	WAUGH–RING warring

Hear it: Track 48. Now if you're up for the challenge, listen to this paragraph then try it for yourself. Get the vowel in these pairs to sound the same. We have marked the pairs in bold:

> Looking into a **big mirror,** I **dressed** in **terror,** as I put on **fat Harry's** hat. I liked it a **lot,** and was **sorry** I hadn't asked him for it. I didn't like the **thought** of **warring** with him, so I took it off. I was in **such** a **hurry** to **start** out on this **starry** night.

> *We recently watched a North American documentary about a Black Bear that we were convinced was called 'Big Hairy'. That was the 'R' Colouring pulling the vowel out of shape; his name was in fact Big Harry!*

L Effect

In a New Standard English Accent the 'L' only affects the **GOAT** vowel.

In some accents when a vowel is followed by a dark 'L' (see 'L' in *Major Players*, pages 104-107), the whole shape may change. As the back of the tongue rises up for the 'L' the vowel shape gets pulled back with it!

There is only one vowel in a New Standard English Accent that *is* affected by the 'L' and that is the GOAT vowel. In fact, if it doesn't affect it you could sound old-fashioned.

Whenever the GOAT vowel is followed by a dark 'L' it changes shape, giving a Neutral Standard English Accent two distinct versions: GOAT = UH–OO and GOAL = O–OO.

Compare the vowels in the words *goat* and *goal*, first spoken in Traditional RP, then in a New Standard English Accent. That's the L Effect!

Hear it: Track 49.

goat   goal x2

The goat was in goal x2

In a NSEA the L Effect remains on the GOAT vowel when the syllable after L starts with a consonant:

Hear It: Track 49.

goat–go**al**   boat–bo**l**der   soak–so**l**dier

But when the next sound is a vowel it may disappear and the vowel then reverts to the GOAT vowel, though this is becoming less common.

Hear it: Track 50. Listen to these two examples:

1. Keeping the new GOAL vowel: O-OO

   Boat–Bowl–Bowler Goat–Goal–Goalie Stoat–Stole–Stolen

2. Reverting to the GOAT vowel: UH-OO

   Boat–Bowl–Bowler Goat–Goal–Goalie Stoat–Stole–Stolen

If your accent *doesn't* have an L Effect, you may actually need to practise it, but only on this vowel!

In accents that use a substitute 'W' such as many London accents, strong Glaswegian and some South Western English accents, the effect can be even stronger and affect many of the vowel shapes. If this is true of your own accent your tongue may need to practise making a clear vowel shape followed by a dark 'L'.

Hear It: Track 51. Listen to the following pairs of words then go through them yourself, being sure to make the vowel sounds the same before adding the dark 'L'.

KIT	KILL		RAFT	MORALE
HEAD	HELL		DOT	DOLL
MUTT	MULL		OUGHT	ALL
FOOT	FULL		FACE	FAIL
FOOD	FOOL		MICE	MILE
FEET	FEEL		BOYS	BOIL
GIRD	GIRL		HOUSE	HOWL
HAT	HAL			

Hear It: Track 52. If you find this challenging, listen to this paragraph then have a go yourself. Be sure to get the vowel in each of the following pairs to sound the same.

> **Beth** was quite a **Belle**. In her **lipstick** she was dressed to **kill**. Her **lot** as a **doll** was to **strut** about and not be **dull**. She thought she looked **good** as she **pulled** on her **boob-tube**, the **fool**! **Fleece** would **feel** much warmer. The **nurse** told the **girl** it was a common **trap**. '**Shall** we run you a **bath** to raise your **morale**? Your **face** looks so **pale**. It will be worth the **price**,' she **smiled**. She gave her no **choice**, and as she **boiled** the water Beth let **out** a **howl**.

4

Stressed or Unstressed?

Vowels are not always stressed (unlike us!). Sometimes it can be the vowel in those little unstressed syllables that makes all the difference to your Standard English Accent. Here are a few rules addressing some of the most common issues.

commA–lettER: Tiny though they may be, these little endings can make or break the authentic sound of your New Standard English Accent. In a Neutral Standard English Accent the sound for these little endings is a mid-central vowel, found on the midpoint on the map. It has no 'shape' as such, just the sound of the mouth in its neutral setting (see page 25).

Hear It: Track 53.

gather   writer   anger   India   Diana   yoga

Being Non-Rhotic (see pages 43-48) all Standard English Accents use exactly the same sound for both of these unstressed endings.

The sound they use is often referred to by phoneticians as a schwa. Schwa is defined as a 'mid-central neutral vowel'. The main quality of a schwa, unlike all other vowels, is that it has no shape as such, it is simply the sound the mouth makes when it returns to its neutral setting. This is all very well, but of course, not every accent's neutral setting produces a 'mid-central neutral vowel', any more than every accent's Foundations produce the same hesitation sound (see page 25), so it is essential to hear and feel the difference between your own commA–lettER sound (or schwa) and that of the Neutral Standard English Accent.

The schwa can also be heard in unstressed syllables at the start and in the middle of words too, such as:

above   another   special   government

Hear It and *Feel It: Track 54.* Listen to the schwa first as a whispered shape, then in the words commA and lettER, and then in this sentence. Use the sentence to practise it.

Diana was concerned that Peter the actor's idea was to write a letter for her brother the worker

---

TOP TIPS FOR NORTH AMERICANS

Be sure to make the sound on your lettER words match EXACTLY the sound on your commA words. They are rhyming pairs! (Now you know why so many English people add an 'R' to the commA words when doing their North American accents. They just want to make them rhyme!) This tiny sound must be made without a hint of an 'R'!

---

happY:

Unlike older Standard English Accents and Northern accents, the *New* Standard English Accent uses a slightly shortened FLEECE vowel for these 'Y' endings. This has developed since around the 1970s, before which you could hear the KIT vowel in all varieties, or even a commA vowel!

Hear It: Track 55.

Pre-1970s happy coffee movie

Post-1970s happy coffee movie

What does your own accent do? commA vowel? DRESS vowel? KIT vowel? FLEECE vowel? It may seem like a small change, but it is very significant. If

---

How To Do Standard English Accents

you don't use a FLEECE vowel, practise this paragraph using the FLEECE vowel for all the 'Y' endings.

Hear It: Track 56.

Bill**y** and Mar**y** were happ**y** to see the mov**ie**, 'When Harr**y** Met Sall**y**.' Bill**y** had a coff**ee,** and Mar**y** bought a pastr**y**.

priv**ATE,** hors**ES,** word endings: commA or KIT vowel?

These little endings have changed over time. In older varieties they all had the KIT vowel, but nowadays in a NSEA some are still KIT but some are commA. So which are which? Here are some guidelines:

Hear It: Track 57.

Use commA in:

- toil**ET** (bracelet, pamphlet, etc.)
- priv**ATE** (climate, etc.)
- probl**EM** (system, Blenheim, etc.)
- kind**NESS** (countless, business, etc.)

Use KIT in:

- hors**ES** (foxes, daises, marries, etc.)
- wast**ED** (landed, excited, etc.)
- long**EST** (biggest, forest, etc.)
- act**IVE** (massive, etc.)
- pock**ET** (biscuit, planet)
- coll**EGE** (sausage, baggage, package, etc.)
- surf**ACE** (office)

'Cons, Coms and Obs' words: Schwa or LOT vowel?

OK, Northerners (and some Americans) take note! You may think these all have the LOT vowel but for a New Standard English Accent this is not the case. Some words have LOT, but some have a commA vowel, or schwa.

So how do you know which to do when? Read on…

In words with two syllables:

NOUNS: stress the first syllable, and use the LOT vowel:
CONduct   COMmune   OBject

VERBS: stress the second syllable, and use the schwa:
conDUCT   comMUNE   obJECT

But in multisyllabic words:

Use LOT if the very next syllable is *un*stressed:
CONseQUENCE   COMpliCATE   OBsoLETE

But use a commA vowel, or schwa, if the very next syllable is *stressed*.
conVEnient   comMUnicate   obJECtify

Can you work out which words use the LOT vowel and which use the commA vowel, or schwa in this paragraph?

Communication in the commune was complicated but completely competent. All the members were compassionate and committed, but observing the old rules was tricky for the more obstinate and obtuse, as they thought them obsolete. Consequently, the more conservative members were concerned that good conduct was obeyed and that everyone conducted themselves with consideration.

Hear It: Track 58. Have a listen and see if you were right!

TOP TIPS FOR NORTH AMERICANS

There are two small sounds that can easily trip up your Standard English Accents if you're not careful. Read on to see what they are!

The first is the unstressed final syllable in words such as *gentlemen*, *basement*.

In North American accents the surrounding nasal sounds colour the vowel and pull it into more of a KIT shape.

gentleMIN   placeMINT

In Standard English Accents there is no nasal colouring and the vowel used is a commA vowel, or schwa.

gentleMUN   placeMUNT

Then there are those words that are *usually* unstressed and spoken with a commA vowel, or schwa, such as *of, from, what, was* and be*cause*. North American accents may use the STRUT vowel when they are stressed, but Standard English Accents the LOT vowel.

Hear It: Track 59.
Of: 'Were you afraid **of** him?' 'There was nothing to be afraid **of**.'
From: 'Who is that **from**?' 'It's from Jan.'
Was: 'Who **was** that?' 'That was Edda.'
Because: 'Just because you say so?' 'Yes, be**cause** I say so!'

5

THE BITE

IN THIS CHAPTER...

We look at the impact of **consonants** on your New Standard English Accent.

We will introduce five **Major Players** that can make or break *any* accent:

'R'   'L'   'H'   'NG'   'TH'

and we will show you the patterns of **how** and **when** to do each of them in a Neutral Standard English Accent.

We will also explore the **Major Issues** that can affect the quality of consonants;

- **Voice, Place and Manner** (how they are made)

- **Consonant Collisions** (what happens when consonants collide with each other)

- **The Glottal Stop** (the invisible consonant replacer)

...and finally we look at a small but crucial detail of when to use a 'consonant in vowel's clothing' that we call '**YOO**'.

THE MAJOR PLAYERS

R L H NG TH

How: A Bending Free 'R'

When: *All* Standard English Accents are Non-Rhotic, so 'R' is only said when followed by a vowel sound!

How To Do a Bending Free 'R'

Hear It: Track 60.

Margaret Linda and Gerry asked Peter if Roland started with 'R'

Hear It: Track 61.

Now hear it in these individual words:

bring   right   grew   lorry   Harry   hero

See It:

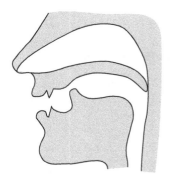

Feel It:

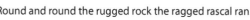

- Curl the tip of your tongue up towards your gum-ridge, without actually touching it.
- Keep it curling up and add your voice to this shape.
- Focus the sound onto the gum-ridge.
- The cheeks may pull in a little to support the shape.

Now practise using the free 'R' (only when followed by a vowel!) with these sentences:

Round and round the rugged rock the ragged rascal ran.

Bring the lorry round the back and raise the retail price.

COMMON MISTAKES

Too Weak: Substitute 'Rs'

In an 'R' substitute, the tongue doesn't move *at all*: instead, the tongue stays flat and the bottom lip lifts up to the top front teeth, almost forming a kind of 'V' or 'W'. You may be familiar with the terms 'weak R' or 'rabbity R'.

 See it: Weak 'R'

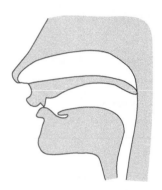

Too Strong: Retroflex/Bunched

In some accents the 'R' is made with a lot more muscularity than the Bending Free 'R'; the 'R' of many American accents is a bunched molar 'R' while the 'R' of Northern Ireland is Retroflex.

 See it: Molar 'R'

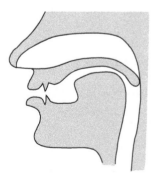 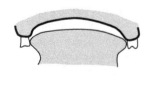

See it: Retroflex 'R'

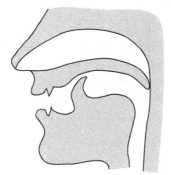

Tapping

A common error is to tap the 'R', giving the accent a very old-fashioned quality (see Part Two for older upper-class varieties, pages 137-200). In a tapped 'R' the tongue is not free, but actually makes contact with the gum-ridge, a little like a quick, light 'D' or 'L'.

See it: Tapped 'R'

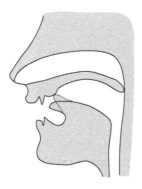

5

R L H NG TH

How: The 'L' can be both light and dark.

When: The light 'L' is only used if it is followed by a vowel sound.

- At the beginning of a word: Look Light
- Separating syllables: Toilet Silly
- On the end of a word if the *next* word starts with a vowel:

    Hill and dale   Fall over

The dark 'L' is used everywhere else!

- On the end of a word where no vowel follows it: *Hill*
- Before a consonant sound: *Field*

Hear It: *Track 62.*
Larry the *l*azy *l*amb *sl*ept peacefully in the field until hailstones fe**ll**

How To Do a Light 'L'

See It: The essential quality of a light 'L' is that *only the front of the tongue* is used to make it.

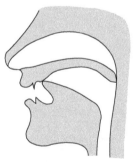

The 'lightness' is variable from 'quite light' to 'extremely light'. This will depend on how much of the front of the tongue makes contact: the less tongue used, the 'lighter' the sound!

Look in the mirror...

- Stick your tongue out and point it up to the middle of your top lip.
- See the way the tongue narrows, points and curls up.
- Keeping the shape, draw the tongue into the mouth and place the pointy tip onto the gum-ridge.

● Keep your tongue as pointy as you can. Avoid a rounded or flat contact.

Feel It: Hold this shape.

● Feel the open space at the back of your mouth and the tensing of the front of the tongue.

● Breathe out through this shape, thinking the vowel 'EE'.

● Add your voice to this shape and you have a light 'L'!

Hear It: Track 63. Listen to the 'EE'-like quality in this light 'L'.

● Now practise getting your tongue to and from this position:

Lee   Loo   Lah

How To Do a Dark 'L'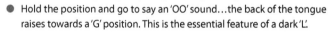

See It: The essential quality of a dark 'L' is that as well as the tongue tip touching the gum-ridge, the *back of the tongue is raised towards the soft palate.*

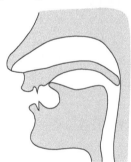

The 'darkness' is variable, from 'quite dark' to 'extremely dark'. This will depend on just how much of the back of the tongue rises. In a New Standard English Accent it is only moderately dark. It is this added muscularity that can make the dark 'L' tricky, especially if your own accent doesn't use it, as is the case in many London accents, for example.

Feel It: Place your tongue tip on your gum-ridge and 'glue' it there.

● Hold the position and go to say an 'OO' sound...the back of the tongue raises towards a 'G' position. This is the essential feature of a dark 'L'.

Hear It: Track 64. Listen to the low resonance of a dark 'L'.

● Now practise getting to this dark 'L' position from these vowels:

eel   ool   all

Now practise combining your light and dark 'L' on the following sentence. We have helped you by indicating all the light 'Ls' in *italics* and all the dark 'Ls' in **bold**:

Whi**l**st *l*arge hai**l**stones fe*ll* and fe**ll**, *l*ovely Mi**l**dred the *l*azy mo**l**e s*l*ept peacefu*ll*y in the fie**l**d

NB. In 'Fell and Fell' the first one becomes light because it is followed by a vowel!

> **TOP TIP**
> One easy way to remember the pattern is:
> **Light 'L'** if the next sound is a vowel.
> **Dark 'L'** if it isn't.

COMMON MISTAKES

One 'L' Accents

Some accents use only light 'Ls' (Southern Welsh, Irish and Newcastle upon Tyne accents for example).

Some use only Dark 'Ls' (Scottish, most Northern English, some New York accents for example).

If your own accent is a one 'L' accent, practise making the new 'L' and using it in all the right places!

Light 'L' plus 'W' Substitute

People whose own accents use a light 'L' before vowels but a 'W' substitute before consonants, or in final positions (London and West Midlands accents for example) often struggle to make a dark 'L' in these positions, and instead replace their 'W' substitute with a light 'L'. This can make them sound Southern Welsh, or Irish, or it can give their articulation a lightly babyish quality.

Take time to train the tongue first of all in how to make a dark 'L', and then practise using it in the right places.

Hear it: Track 52. Use these word pairs from page 94, the L Effect, to practise.

L

TOP TIPS FOR NORTH AMERICANS

1. Although most North American accents have two 'Ls', the one they use before a vowel is not a light 'L'. Instead it's a slightly lighter dark 'L' (or a medium 'L', if you prefer). For this reason it is always necessary to lighten the 'L' before a vowel.

2. Pay particular attention to words such as William, Gillian, million etc. American accents tend to make these 'Ls' dark and follow them with 'Y'.

Will-yam   Gill-yon   mill-yon

In the New Standard English Accent these are light 'Ls' followed by the KIT vowel!

Will–i–am   Gill–i–an   mill–i–on

3. Deep South and AAVE (African American Vernacular English) accents may use a medium 'L' before a vowel and a 'W' substitute everywhere else. In these cases learn a light 'L' to use before vowels, and use your own medium 'L' everywhere else!

5

R L **H** NG TH

How: A puff of air

When: Always, unless a syllable has *no weight at all*.

Hear It: Track 65. Harry Hobson had a holiday in Hawaii.

Take this sentence, for example:

I'll go with him

If the stress is on the word *him*, that 'H' must be said:

*I'll go with **h**im*

If the stress is put on the word *go* then the 'H' *may* get dropped (though it doesn't have to, and only if the speech is rapid!)

I'll go with 'im

See www.howtodoaccents.com for other examples of where 'H' can be dropped in *Arthur the Rat*.

If you are naturally an 'H'-doer, you will follow this pattern too, but if you are not, getting that 'H' to make an appearance may need a little concentration.

How To Do an 'H'

See It: In Shaw's *Pygmalion*, Henry Higgins teaches Eliza Doolittle to put her 'Hs' in by speaking in front of a candle flame. As she pushes out the puff of 'H', she can see the flame flicker. Not a bad technique: try it!

You could also use a mirror, or a pane of glass, and watch it steam up as you push the 'H' puff of air onto it.

Feel It: Put one hand on your stomach and the other in front of your mouth.

Pant like a puppy. One hand will feel the muscles that do the pushing, the other will feel the warm air. That's an 'H'!

Although this is pretty simple, it takes practice to drop this action into the midst of speech when you're not used to it. Try these phrases:

I hope so. I hope you have.

I hope you have your hat.

We have to. We have to hide.

We have to hide in here.

COMMON MISTAKES

'H'-droppers sometimes aren't sure if a word starts with an 'H' or not! They may think they dropped an 'H', when in fact they didn't! This can lead to a phenomenon known as 'hyper-correction' when they put in an 'H' which should never be there! Ask an 'H'-dropper how to say the letter Aitch: they may well answer Haitch! If this is you, pay attention to the spelling: no 'H'? Then don't say one!

R L H **NG** TH

How: Soft release.

When: *All* **word endings**. (Also *within* words that are built from activities e.g. to sing–singer, to bang–banger.)

Hear It: Track 66.

The smiling singer was singing for the king.

In some *other* accents 'NG' endings may be soft, but they may also be hard or dropped, depending on what *type* of word it is!
The kinds of words that end in 'NG' fit into two groups.

1. 'NG' Words

- 'NG' nouns (people, objects) – a gong; a ring.
- 'NG' verbs (doing words) – to hang; to bring.
- 'NG' adjectives (describing words) – long; strong.

In ALL Standard English Accents these have a soft 'NG'.

2. 'ING' Words

- 'ING' verb endings (continual doing words) – running; laughing.

In a New Standard English Accent these also have a soft 'NG'.

5

The *only* time a Standard English Accent uses a hard 'NG' is when it appears *within* words *not* built from activities, such as: *'finger', 'angle',* (and all -NGLE words), *'strongest'* (and all -NGEST words), *'angrily', 'language',* etc. Here the first syllable ends with the soft 'NG' and the second syllable starts with a 'G';

fing–**g**er   ang–**g**le   strong–**g**est   ang–**g**rily   lang–**g**uage

If you want to check, ask yourself… 'Can I Fing? Can I Ang? Can I Strong? Can I Lang?' If the answer is 'No', then use a hard 'NG'!

How To Do a Soft NG

See it:

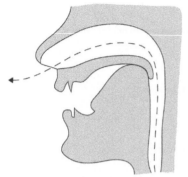

The back of the tongue is up on the soft palate and the sound goes into the nose.

The back of the tongue then has a soft release as it drops down silently.

Hear It: and *Feel It:* Practise with these sentences, using soft 'NG' throughout.

The si**ng**er was si**ng**ing for the ki**ng**.
As she was si**ng**ing and skippi**ng** alo**ng** to the so**ng**, the ki**ng** sa**ng** alo**ng**!

COMMON MISTAKES

Are you a hard 'NG' user?
Make sure you don't squeeze, click or bounce. The soft 'NG' has a soft gliding release. This may feel as if you haven't finished the sound!
Are you an 'ING' dropper?

Make sure you use the BACK of the tongue for the end of the word SINGING, just as you do on all the other words in the sentence!

R L H NG **TH**

How: Standard 'TH'

When: Everywhere!

Hear It: Track 67. That's my brother with a Thermos of Matthew's broth.

'TH' is a sound that other accents love to have fun with. There are in fact *two* 'TH' sounds in English, one made with voice and one without.

A standard 'TH', as used in all Standard English Accents, has three features:

- ● Voiced or Voiceless (buzzy or breathy)
- ● Dental (tongue tip on the teeth)
- ● Fricative (air escaping with friction/hiss)

How To Do a 'TH'

See it:

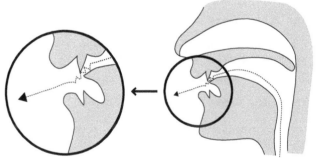

- ● The tongue tip almost touches the underside of all the top front teeth
- ● The air is released with friction
- ● Look in the mirror to see your tongue in the position

Feel It: Coat the underside of all the top front teeth *gently* with your tongue tip. Push air gently between the tongue and teeth and feel the air escaping. The tongue must stay soft to do this!

Hear It: Track 68. Listen to the standard 'THs', first on their own and then in sentences, then have a go yourself.

Voiceless: THHH   It's a thick pathetic broth

Voiced: thhhh   Look at those brothers bathe

Hear the air escaping with a breathy hissing sound. That's the friction! That's your **standard** *voiceless* 'TH'.

Add voice to it and **hear** the buzzy hissing sound escaping. That's your **standard** *voiced* 'TH'.

Feel your face, neck and chest as you add voice to feel the vibrations resonating.

COMMON MISTAKES

1. 'F'/'V': Replacing Voiceless 'TH' with 'F':
Replacing Voiced 'TH' with 'V' (though *not* at the beginning of words).

Think–Fink	Matthew–Maffew	Bath–Baff
Brother–Bruvver	With–wiv	

2. 'F'/'D'/'V': As above, but more contemporary/urban is the replacement of initial voiced 'TH' with 'D':

Think–Fink	Matthew–Maffew	Bath–Baff
That–Dat	Brother–Bruvver	With–Wiv

3. 'T'/'D': Replacing Voiceless 'TH' with a 'T'-like sound and voiced with a 'D'-like sound (common in Southern Irish and Caribbean accents):

Think–Tink	Matthew–Mattew	With–Wid/Wit
That–Dat	Brother–Brudder	Bath–Batt

There is currently an *epidemic* of 'F'/'V' replacement sweeping the English-speaking world, making this a feature of *many* accents of English, but not Standard English Accents (yet, though some of the New Wave are beginning to adopt it!).

For some people who have this as a feature the standard 'TH' will be a *completely new* sound/tongue action for the tongue to make, for others the *tongue* may know how to do it, but getting the brain to remember will be another matter.

Correcting the *initial* sound (the sound at the beginning of a word) can be relatively straightforward; it is the ones in the middle, and especially the end, that can easily get overlooked, and if it happens to be on the end of a seemingly small linking word.

THE MAJOR PLAYERS CHECKLIST

'R' Margaret, Linda and Gerry asked Peter if Roland started with 'R'.
'L' Larry the lamb slept peacefully in the field until hailstones fell.
'H' Harry Hobson had a holiday in Hawaii.
'NG' The smiling singer was singing for the king.
'TH' That's my brother with a thermos of Matthew's broth.

NSEA

'R' Bending and free
'L' Light and dark combination
'H' Not dropped
'NG' Soft everywhere, never dropped
'TH' Standard everywhere

YOU

'R' What kind of 'R' do you use: tap, bunch, curl, bend?
'L' Do you have one or two kinds of 'L'? What kind(s) of 'L'?
'H' Are you an 'H'-dropper, or an 'H'-doer?
'NG' What kind of 'NG' do you have? Is it ever dropped?
'TH' What kind of 'TH' do you use? Standard, Plosive, 'T'/'D' substitutes, 'F'/'V' substitutes?

5

If any of the above are different from the NSEA patterns, focus on that Major Player until you are confident and fluent in making and using it. Remember, it can make or break your accent!

MAJOR ISSUES

Voice, Place and Manner

Every time you make a consonant you make three decisions:

- How much vocal vibration is in the sound (**Voice**).
- Where in the mouth the contact is made (**Place**).
- The way in which the sound is released (**Manner**).

Change one or more of these three elements and the quality of the consonant will change dramatically, which can make or break a good Standard English Accent.

There are 24 consonants in a Standard English Accent, each with its own combination of **Voice, Place** and **Manner**. Depending on your own accent some will be straightforward, others more challenging. The biggest challenges have been covered in **Major Players**, but sometimes the devil really is in the detail!

The chart below shows the Standard English consonants, using the letter of the alphabet that best represents them, and a simple word in which they appear.

- **Voice**: voiced sounds are shown in **bold**.
- **Place**: is shown across the top of the chart.
- **Manner**: is described down the side of the chart.

PLACE / MANNER	Lips	Lip and Teeth	Tongue and Teeth	Gum-ridge	Behind Gum-ridge	Roof of mouth	Soft Palate	Throat
Plosive Air flow held back then suddenly released as a firm explosion	'P' **'B'** pip **bib**			'T' **'D'** tat **dad**			'K' **'G'** kick **gig**	
Fricative Air escaping continually, like a 'hiss'		'F' **'V'** fan **van**	'TH' **'TH'** thick **this**	'S' **'Z'** Sue **zoo**	'SH' **'ZH'** mesh **measure**			'H' hay
Affricate Starts like a plosive but turns into a fricative!					'CH' **'DJ'** chew **Jew**			
Nasal Sound diverted down the nose	**'M'** **mum**			**'N'** **nun**			**'NG'** **song**	
Approximant Articulators brought almost together, then sprung apart	**'W'** **we**				'R' raw	**'Y'** **you**		
Lateral Sound released from the sides of the tongue				'L' lull				

NB. The five **Major Players** are shown in grey.

Voice: devoicing

One major issue that can ruin all your hard work is the habit of *de*voicing the voiced consonants in a Standard English Accent. Devoicing can be a real problem for actors, as it takes away so much of the resonance and richness from the overall quality of the voice.

As you can see on the chart, there are eight *pairs* of consonants that share the same place, and the same manner of release, but one is voiced (using vocal vibrations) and the other is voiceless (using only air). The eight pairs are:

Hear It: Track 69.

- 'B'–'P'
- 'D'–'T'
- 'G'–'K'
- 'V'–'F'

- 'TH'–'TH'
- 'Z'–'S'
- 'ZH'–'SH'
- 'DJ'–'TCH'

Feel It:

Copy what you hear, going from 'B' to 'P' then 'D' to 'T' and so on. Put your fingers on your voice box as you do this and feel the vibrations switching on and off.

Hear It: Track 70 and 71.

Now listen to this sentence being spoken twice: the first time with standard voicing, the second time with voice removed.

> Don't allow your **vivid** imagination to lead you to **believe that** Jan **loves** cats and **dogs**: it's a **delusion.**

You can hear what a difference devoicing makes! Have a go yourself, adding and removing voice. You will *feel* the difference too. The tongue is softer and springier in the voiced sounds, sharper and tighter in the voiceless ones.

If you have a habit of devoicing, or if it is a feature of your own accent, we strongly recommend you practise the new sensations and sounds. You can refer to our list of speech books on page 232 for further reading and practice material.

> **TOP TIP**
>
> Devoicing can also be associated with a splashy release and changes in placement, so be sure to check the place and manner as well.

Voice: adding voice

Voice can also be added to otherwise voiceless consonants. The consonant most commonly affected by this is 'T'. Many contemporary speakers, considered to have Standard English Accents, have begun using a voiced version of a 'T' (in other words a 'D'!) between some vowels, perhaps in order to keep the flow of voice going in rapid or informal speech, maybe to sound more London, or perhaps because of the influence of American…or possibly a bit of all three…

 See it:

better go home = bedder go home

get a big car = gedda big car

got to move on = godda move on

Beware! For many accents, such as North American and Liverpudlian, this is a necessary feature, but for a NSEA 'you're bedder off' avoiding it, unless you are playing a more contemporary character, possibly working in the media, or politics, in which case maybe look at **Sloane Rangers** on page 191 or the **New Wave** on page 201.

> **TOP TIPS**
>
> If you are from the Midlands or the North of England beware of this innocent looking little word; it has voicing issues that can really give the game away:
>> *US*
>
> In your own accent you are likely to use a voiced 'Z' in this word: *'UZZ'*
> In a NSEA it has a voiceless 'S': *'USS'*!
>
> If you are from Scotland, Ireland, Canada and parts of the US (and maybe other places we don't know about?), watch out for this innocent looking little word:
>> *With*
>
> In your own accent you are likely to use a voiceless 'TH'.
> In a NSEA it has a voiced 'TH'!

Place

Technically any consonant can be affected by a change in placement, but the standard consonant that is by far the most dramatically affected is, you guessed it…'T'.

Feel It: Making a Standard 'T'

- Release your lower jaw, making a space at least as big as your little finger between the front teeth.
- Raise the tip of the tongue and place it on the gum-ridge, immediately behind your upper teeth.
- Without involving the jaw, press and release the tongue as your breath expels.
- Add voice to the above and you have a 'D'.

If the tongue flattens, the jaw closes, the tongue slides forward onto the teeth or the tip rolls down behind the bottom teeth, the quality of this sound will clearly be affected. What you are aiming for is a clean tap, without too much of a 'high hat' cymbal sound to it.

> **TOP TIP**
>
> The setting of the jaw and the tongue will have a knock-on effect on the placement of consonants. A tongue that sits with the tip curled down and the body rolled forward will tend to pull the consonants forward with it. A jaw that holds the teeth close together will make tongue lifts tricky. But the reverse is also true…get those consonants placed well and it will really inform your setting!

5

Manner of Release

There are six manners of release used in Standard English Accents (see chart on page 114). The most common problem that can affect the quality of your NSEA is turning plosives into fricatives. Effectively this means that instead of a firm contact and a clean explosive bounce there is a soft contact and a 'splashy' release of the sound. This is a great feature of a Liverpool accent, but not so good if you're doing a Standard English Accent! And guess which sound is most obviously affected…'T'!

Hear It: Track 72.

Listen to the difference between the splashy (fricative) 'T' and the clean 'T'.

What a to-do to die today at a minute or two to two.

So, look back at the chart and firm up those plosives.

Consonant Collisions

Of course, consonants don't stand alone in a word. Life isn't that simple.

Consonants often collide or cluster in the English language: sometimes within a word, as in '**tr**ou**ble**'; and sometimes when two words collide, as in 'o**ld r**at' or 'coul**d n**ever'. This can lead to three common problems: dropping, crunching, and over-egging.

Dropping

Some accents like to make life much simpler by *dropping* consonants out of a cluster.

See It:

Look at these examples of consonants getting dropped from consonant collisions.

Where have all the 'Ts' gone?

> It's the best people I most miss – Is a bess people I mohs miss

And the 'K'?

> I asked–I Ahst

And the 'L'?

> Alright–Awright

In a New Standard English Accent the *only* consonant that often gets dropped and *only* in informal and contemporary speech is a 'T' immediately before another consonant, where it is replaced by a Glottal Stop (see page 124).

> e.g. grea**t** gang ge**t** back foo**t** ball

Hear It: Track 73.

Listen to the way the NSEA speaker drops the 'T' in the phrase '*may not come down*' and replaces it with a Glottal Stop.

Crunching

Some accents *crunch* the consonants in the cluster together. They may make a completely new sound from those in the cluster, and sometimes they change a quality of the first sound to pre-empt the next one.

Try this phrase:

> How do you get to London Bridge?

Some of you may be saying 'How joo get to Londom Bridge'.

- The 'D'–'Y' of 'do you' becomes 'J' (new sound).
- The 'N' of London moves onto the lips in readiness for the 'B' and so becomes an 'M' (changed sound).

If not, have a go at doing it. That's what we mean by crunching.

Now, it is worth pointing out that English does have a long history of crunching, especially where a 'Y' sound is involved.

Look at a word such as *'nature'*, for example. There would have been a time that this was pronounced naytyuh, but it hasn't been said that way in a Standard English Accent for a very long time!

Over the course of the 20ᵗʰ century this process has really speeded up. Daniel Jones (he of the Daniel Jones pronunciation dictionary) pronounced *actual* as actyoo-ul, but nowadays that would be perceived as mannered or artificial in a Standard English Accent.

But there is a set of crunches that are not (yet?) considered standard and can still destroy your Standard English Accent:

Hear It: Track 74. Listen to the following, first crunched then uncrunched!

'DY': Did **y**ou do your **du**ty? (The 'DY' crunches to 'J', as in Judge)

'TY': I'll pass that **tu**na over to you. (The 'TY' crunches to 'CH')

'STY': I guessed **y**ou were st**u**pid. (The 'STY' crunches to 'SH'–'CH')

'DR': I had a **dr**eam about dr**u**ids. (The 'DR' crunches to 'JR')

'TR': The **tr**ain ran out of pe**tr**ol. (The 'TR' crunches to 'CHR')

'STR': The **str**eet was ext**r**emely st**r**aight. (The 'STR' crunches to 'SH'–'CHR')

The first three 'Y' crunches are well on their way to becoming standard, especially in contemporary and informal speech, though they're not quite there yet, and the 'R' crunches are making progress too, but the last one has a long way to go before it is even close to becoming standard; so if this is one of your habits, it is really worth uncrunching.

One way to teach your tongue to uncrunch the 'STR' collision is to work through the word backwards.

1 REET	1 REMELY	1 RAIGHT
2 TREET	2 TREMELY	2 TRAIGHT
3 STREET	3 STREMELY	3 STRAIGHT
	4 KSTREMELY	
	5 EKSTREMELY	

Another way is to plot the journey of the tongue as it goes through the sequence. In the crunched version the journey is:

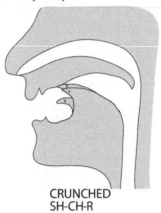

**CRUNCHED
SH-CH-R**

Whereas in the uncrunched version it is:

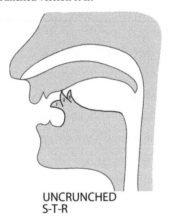

**UNCRUNCHED
S-T-R**

And once you have mastered this movement, having practised it slowly and carefully, try using it in this paragraph:

> The sporty student was struggling while training on the running tracks. 'I'm strong enough!' he thought, and took a tube into town. There he traipsed through the streets with a dubious attitude, drinking drams of whiskey and whistling stupid tunes. Extraordinary!

See www.howtodoaccents.com for other examples of 'DY', 'TY', 'STY', 'DR', 'TR' and 'STR' combinations in *Arthur the Rat*.

Over-egging

It may surprise some people to learn that, in a New Standard English Accent (in fact in *all* varieties of Standard English Accent), it is sometimes absolutely correct *not* to fully articulate all the consonants. Indeed, to do so reveals the speaker's accent as fake or phoney, or as Clifford Turner puts it in his book *Voice and Speech in the Theatre*:

> *would be ludicrous…absurd and a travesty of the truth.*

That may sound a little harsh; we prefer to call it 'over-egging the pudding'.

Instead the following rule applies:

When a sequence of colliding consonants is made in the *same place* in the mouth, hold the tongue in place through the first consonant, into the second, and only release when the *last consonant* is made in that place.

Hear It: Track 75.

This can happen within words:

topmost   background

And between words:

steep bank   get down   had tuna   get Sam   had supper   back garden

Here are some examples from *Arthur the Rat* (see page 225), shown with the phrase number in brackets. Listen out for this feature in our various speakers' readings of this passage

(8) said to him

(22) caught sight

(31) immediate decision

(33) said to himself

(34) make up my mind

(36) next day

(39) quite dead

This results in an *ESSENTIAL* feature of all but the youngest Standard English Accents, known in the phonetic world as '**Nasal and Lateral Plosions**'. Sounds uncomfortable? Well, if you're not used to doing them, they can be!

Nasal Plosions: 'TN' 'DN'

As our friend Clifford Turner puts it:

> *a vowel should **not** be inserted between an explosive and a following nasal.*

In other words...

When the consonants 'TN' and 'DN' collide, either within a word, or between two words, the tongue goes up to make a 'T' or 'D' on the gum-ridge, holds its position and then the soft palate drops to release the sound down the nose as an 'N'. **There is no release at all between the two consonants!**

Hear It: Track 76.

'TN'	'DN'
button	hidden
get Nancy	had nuts

See It:

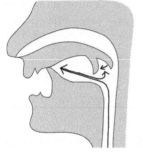

When it happens within a word, there is no vowel between the consonants; instead the 'N' takes the weight of the syllable (syllabic 'N'). Here are some examples:

'TN'	'DN'
rotten	garden
kitten	wooden
frighten	Eden

When it happens between words the 'T' or 'D' is held over and released into the 'N' of the next word. Here are some more examples:

'TN'	'DN'
sit nicely	odd noise
wet nose	red nose

Lateral Plosions: 'TL' 'DL'

Clifford Turner again:

> *a vowel should **not** be inserted between an explosive and…a following 'L'.*

In other words…

When the consonants 'TL' and 'DL' collide, either within a word, or between two words, the tongue tip goes up to make a 'T' or 'D' on the gum-ridge, holds its position and then **the sides of the tongue** drop down to release the sound as an 'L'. **There is no release at all between the two consonants!**

Hear It: Track 77.

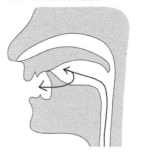

'TL'	'DL'
little	cuddle
get Lionel	had lunch

See It:

When it happens within a word, there is no vowel between the consonants; instead the 'L' takes the weight of the syllable (syllabic 'L'). Here are some examples:

'TL'	'DL'
kettle	middle
bottle	waddle
battle	needle

When it happens between words, the 'T' or 'D' is held over and released into the 'L' of the next word. Here are some examples:

'TL'	'DL'
cat litter	red legs

So those are Nasal and Lateral Plosions. If your mouth has never made these moves before, it may feel, and even sound, quite peculiar when you first learn them. Maybe you prefer to insert a vowel between the colliding consonants, sounding something like this:

'littul' and 'rottun'

5

Not such a crime, you may think, but according to Clifford Turner it is:

both childish and uneducated.

Blimey! That may be a bit strong, but nevertheless, this really *isn't* what to do in a New Standard English Accent: Nasal and Lateral Plosions are a must!

There are many examples of Nasal and Lateral Plosions in *Arthur the Rat* for you to listen to and practise. See www.howtodoaccents.com for a highlighted list.

The Glottal Stop (ʔ)

Although a Glottal Stop can be heard regularly in speakers of English from all over the country (usually to replace or reinforce a 'P', 'T' or 'K'), it is only very rarely heard in a Standard English Accent, and then on only one sound. Can you guess which one? Of course, it's Mr. 'T'.

Nowadays it has become the norm in a Neutral Standard English Accent to use a Glottal Stop in place of a 'T' when the sound immediately following it is another consonant, either between words or within a word:

For example: *quite good* = quiʔgood   *football* = fooʔbll

But it is never used before a vowel:

get away   quite alright   better

though this can be heard in many New Wave speakers (see pages 201-210). The Glottal Stop is one of those features that has been steadily growing over the last 60 years. In the 1950s it would be more unusual to hear a Glottal Stop before 'R', 'W', 'Y', 'M':

T–R Get real   T–W Get well   T–Y Get you   T–M Get mother

But 60 years later this is considered neutral.

Look at the examples of the possible glottal 'Ts' in *Arthur the Rat* on www.howtodoaccents.com.

> TOP TIP
> Next time you make a 'T', you might want to check it for some major issues...
> • Voice, Place and Manner
> • Drops, Crunches and Over-egging
> And of course, the Glottal Stop!

YOO!

The springing consonant 'Y' can make a special appearance before the vowel sound 'OO'. You may hear it referred to as the 'liquid YOO' or 'YOD'.

There are five possible 'YOO' patterns, depending on your accent:

1 'YOOs' everywhere
2 'YOO' dropping after 'L' and 'S'
3 'YOO' dropping after 'L' and 'S' and crunching after 'T' and 'D'
4 'YOO' dropping after all gum-ridge consonants
5 No 'YOOs' at all!

So which one should you use in a NSEA? You might think it would be the first one, keeping all the 'YOOs', as this may seem 'correct', but in fact, NSEA has gone on a steady journey through the patterns, starting at 1, currently in a mix of 2 and 3, and who knows, maybe going into 4 soon...?

So what are the current rules for a NSEA?

New Standard English Accent: The 'YOO' rules.

'YOO' dropping after *most* 'Ls' and all 'Ss'

Hear it: Track 78.

NSEA:

> Rather than be lewd, he presumed it was his duty to play a suitable tune with enthusiasm.

Never use 'YOO' before an 'S':

suit   suicide

And only rarely use it before an 'L', if it is an 'old-fashioned' word, or one just not used that much:

not in: absolute   deluded   v   possible in: lewd   alluded

But this only applies to stressed syllables. *Keep* the 'YOO' after the 'L' in unstressed syllables:

VALue = valyoo
SALuTAtions = salyootations

But change it to 'SHOO' after the 'S' in unstressed syllables:

TISHoo (tissue)
ISHoo (issue)

5

Listen to this sentence being spoken, keeping *all* the 'YOO' pronunciations:

Hear It: Track 79.

Rather than be lewd, he presumed it was his duty to play a suitable tune with enthusiasm.

NB. 'presumed' may *look* like it has an 'S' in it, but it's said as a 'Z'!

If you think it sounds rather old-fashioned, you'd be right! And it will be the words LEWD and SUIT that did it.

Having said all that, when you listen to our example speakers, you may notice that Standard English Accents are having something of an identity crisis, mixing and matching these patterns as they try to blend in, or keep up to date.

COMMON (AND FATAL!) MISTAKES
Crunching after 'T' and 'D' and 'Z'

If your regional accent is a little stronger, as well as dropping 'YOO' after 'L' and 'S', you may well 'crunch' the 'YOO' after a 'T', 'D' and 'Z' so that **tune** becomes **choon** and **duty** becomes **jooty**, and **presumed** becomes **prezhoomed**

Hear It: Track 80.

Rather than be lewd, he presumed it was his duty to play a suitable tune with enthusiasm.

Practise separating out those crunched consonants, giving them back their separate identities!

Dropping after *all* gum-ridge consonants: 'S', 'Z', 'N', 'T', 'D', 'L' and 'THs'

This is the pattern used by the vast majority of North American accents. In those accents *all* the following words lose the 'YOO' in it, whereas in a NSEA only SUIT and LEWD do.

'S': **suit**   'Z': **presume**   'N': **nude**   'T': **attitude**   'D': **duty**   'L': **lewd**   'TH': **enthuse**

TOP TIP FOR NORTH AMERICANS

It's not that you don't know how to do this sound, as you have it in words like MUSIC and BEAUTIFUL, it's just a case of being sure to use it with those gum-ridge consonants: all of them to sound a little old-fashioned, or just 'Z', 'N', 'T', 'D' and 'TH' to sound contemporary!

See www.howtodoaccents.com for other examples of 'YOOs' in *Arthur the Rat*.

5

THE MAJOR ISSUES CHECKLIST
NSEA

Voice, Place and Manner: This chart shows all the Standard English consonants with their Voice, Place and Manner of Release.

MANNER \ PLACE	Lips	Lip and Teeth	Tongue and Teeth	Gum-ridge	Behind Gum-ridge	Roof of mouth	Soft Palate	Throat
Plosive	'P' 'B'			'T' 'D'			'K' 'G'	
Fricative		'F' 'V'	'TH' 'TH'	'S' 'Z'	'SH' 'ZH'			'H'
Affricate					'CH' 'DJ'			
Nasal	'M'			'N'			'NG'	
Approximant	'W'				'R'	'Y'		
Lateral				'L'				

Consonant Collisions:

- No dropping, except 'T' before another consonant.
- No crunching.
- 'TN', 'DN' (*hidden button*) and 'TL', 'DL' (*middle bottle*) are Nasal and Lateral Plosions.

The Glottal Stop: Only used to replace a 'T' immediately before another consonant.

'YOO': Dropped before most 'Ls' (lewd) and 'Ss' (suitable). Kept everywhere else.

Rather than be lewd he pre**su**med it was his **du**ty to play a **fe**w suitable **tu**nes with ent**hu**siasm.

YOU

Voice, Place and Manner: How does the way you make your consonants compare to the chart above?

Consonant Collisions:

- Do you drop or crunch consonants?
- Do you use Nasal and Lateral Plosions: hidden button – middle bottle

The Glottal Stop: Do you replace or accompany any consonants or words with a Glottal Stop?

'YOO': Do you keep or drop any 'YOOs' from this sentence?

Rather than be lewd he pre**su**med it was his **du**ty to play a **fe**w suitable **tu**nes with ent**hu**siasm.

Identify where your accent has Major Issues that differ from NSEA. Focus on these to be sure your NSEA has its own issues and not yours!

A NOD TO THE OLD WAVE...

This book has so far given actors a route to developing a contemporary standard accent that they can use on stage and screen, in any role where specific indicators of age, gender, race, class, etc. are unwanted. But training of the actor's accent is not a new phenomenon. The accent we have described has moved on some way from the **OLD STAGE STANDARD** accent used by the voices we may associate with the stage actors of the past. In old theatrical training, the actor's accent and voice training were intrinsically woven together. As late as the 1970s and even 1980s in some drama schools, actors were expected to lose their own accent completely as part of their vocal training.

The approach to a standard accent that we have taken is reflected in this quote by the phonetician J.C. Wells:

> *A standard accent is regarded as a standard (or 'norm') not because of any intrinsic qualities it may possess, but because of an arbitrary attitude adopted towards it by society.*
>
> J.C. Wells, 1982.

But in the olden days of theatre training the perception was quite different. There were very grey areas between the concept of a standard accent and the upper-class accent of the time, and between speech training and accent training. The actor was encouraged towards 'beauty' and a 'good sound'.

> *Pleasantness is a matter much more of tone and quality in the voice than of the accent or pronunciation of particular words.*

while on the other hand...

> *Accent...may be regarded as a variation from standard, and, more often than not, a debasement of the sounds attempted.*
>
> *Improved vitality and greater conscious activity on the part of the speech organs will go a long way towards the elimination of accent and a general improvement in speech.*
>
> Gwyneth L. Thurburn, 1959.

The accent of the old RADA- and CSSD-trained actors as heard in the voices of actors such as Sir Laurence Olivier, Sir John Gielgud, Dame Flora Robson and Dame Peggy Ashcroft, cannot be easily separated from the upper-class accents of the period, except in terms of the techniques of voice production that added to the richness of tone and resonance, the clarity of articulation, and the extraordinary use of music to express the movement of thoughts and emotions.

5

The old methods of training persisted with very slight variations into the voices of younger actors trained in both schools and the rep. system such as Sir Ian McKellen, Glenda Jackson, Prunella Scales and Timothy West.

THE FOUNDATIONS

Setting

Jaw: two finger drop, loose jaw muscles, perhaps not so different from NSEA but much more rigorously trained and adhered to!

Pharynx: the throat retracts creating an open space at the back, to resonate rich, warm undertones.

Soft Palate: raised to create space, but still flexible, not tense.

Tongue: as with a NSEA, the back and root of the tongue are soft and released forward. The tongue tip has to lift and curl up more in the increased space, 'T' – setting may be a little bit further back on a tighter spot, 'cupping' the sound.

All the above contribute to creating a *lot* of space in the centre and back of the oral chamber that resonates the lower frequencies of the voice.

Zone

1 and **2.5** and driving up through the bones and cavities at the front of the face and into the facial mask. This adds the bright resonance to the voice.

Tone

Very rich, and full like a cello. Descriptions such as 'plummy' may be used.

As Gwyneth L. Thurburn says in *Voice and Speech*:

> *It is essential to good tone that the hollow spaces of the neck, mouth and nose are free and unimpeded if they are to act properly as resonators of the sound.*
>
> *This freedom is attained by:*
>
> *a) Good breathing*
> *b) Flexibility of all the muscles*
> *c) Sensitiveness to the vibrations*

A certain amount of accessory resonance may be obtained from feeling the sound forward in the face.

The sensation of forward vibration diverts the attention from the throat and helps the sense of projection towards an objective.

Sensation at the back is always harmful, but sensation in front is of the greatest possible value.

Direction

While there is energy in the back of the mouth, the pharynx, soft palate, etc., it is vital to keep the direction of flow driving forward energetically or the tone will become muffled.

THE GROOVE

Tune

The tune of the old stage accent was quite different from the modern sound. The theatrical voice used dramatic swoops through the range and large extensions of stressed vowel lengths. The aim was to achieve a sung quality:

Sing the sentences on a descending scale (eight notes, or five notes) or on one note and then speak them, preserving the sustained tone but introducing varied inflexions.

Gwyneth L. Thurburn

Rhythm

The tune was supported by a strong use of a driving rhythm which can sound quite exaggerated and over-dramatic to modern ears.

THE SHAPES AND BITE

As far as the specifics of the vowel shapes and the bite of the consonants are concerned, this really was based on the upper-class accent of the time, as described in **Imperial Lords and Ladies** (see page 149), with the possible exception of the GOAT and LOT vowels.

GOAT–GOAL: The stage version of this shape was a fairly open, rounded shape, the sound resonating with low frequencies, and closer to a Standard American shape in some ways. A shortened version was also used in unstressed positions in words such as **obey, occasion**, etc. In a New Standard English Accent these would have a schwa.

LOT: This was a little less rounded and more open.

It may be worth pointing out that this accent also formed the basis for the training of actors in North America, and this fact, coupled with influence of the upper-class American accents of the East Coast, explains those wonderful, if somewhat unplaceable mid-Atlantic accents heard in American movies of the 1930s and 1940s.

Hear It: *Track 161.*

These recordings of Mrs Patrick Campbell from 1929 and Mr Beerbohm Tree from 1906 are beautiful examples of the old style.

PART TWO
UPPER-CLASS VARIETIES

6
THE VARIETIES

So, if a New Standard English Accent is not 'Posh', what is?

In Part Two of the book we introduce you to some varieties of Standard English Accent, all of which come from the upper and upper middle classes.

We cannot possibly cover all the idiosyncracies that are thrown up in life, nor do we aim to. We have taken as our models the characters and types found most often in plays and films through the 20th and 21st centuries, to give you a spectrum of possibilities to choose from. Choose the variety that most suits the role you are playing. After all, if you are playing Hamlet, you may not want to sound like BBC Bertie, or if you are playing Lady Bracknell, you may not want to sound like a Sloane Ranger!

Though some of these varieties may share certain features, we decided to write them in such a way that, for the most part, they can stand alone and you can read each as a separate entity without constant cross-referencing. We have also included some suggestions of people, characters and plays that may be useful as reference points for each variety.

The first variety we describe is Traditional RP. This is a catch-all accent that is quite distinct from a New Standard English Accent, and useful if you want a good basis to distinguish you in terms of class and period. Should you be looking for something more 'character-ful' then venture with us as we describe the glories of the **Imperial Lords and Ladies**, the pragmatism of the **Military, Matrons and the Landed Gentry**, the hedonistic **Debs, Dandies and Bright Young Things**, the austerity of the **Wartime Wendies and BBC Berties**, the triumph of the **Sloane Rangers**, and as we finally give a nod to the ever inventive **New Wave**.

TRADITIONAL RP

The FRAME ————————

This is the ideal accent if what you are looking for is a fairly standard, old-fashioned, upper or upper middle class, but not overly eccentric accent. Here we will describe a 'generic' sound, free from overt indicators of character found in the accents of the Imperial Lords and Ladies, Military, Matrons and the Landed gentry, Debs, Dandies and Bright Young Things, or the Wartime Wendies and BBC Berties.

This variety of Standard English pronunciation was born of the accent of the upper classes of the turn of the 20th century, which in turn was influenced by the accents of the Royal Family and associated aristocracy. It may be worth mentioning that from 1714 until the death of Queen Victoria in 1901, the British Royal Family were all from the House of Hanover and many of them spoke only Hanoverian German, or were bilingual in English and Hanoverian German. This will have had a profound effect on their English pronunciation, and you may notice that some of the vowels do have a Germanic quality to them. The accent began to be more formalised in the 1920s and with the establishment of the education system and the BBC, it rapidly became the standard used right through to the 1970s. Many of the middle classes aspired to lose the 'tag' and perceived limitations of their own regional accents and dialects. It was originally called Received Pronunciation or 'RP' for short (the word 'received' being an old-fashioned word meaning 'accepted'), although varieties of it may be referred to as heightened, marked or period RP.

People: Tom Baker, Judi Dench, Joan Hickson, Patricia Hodge, Martin Jarvis, Felicity Kendal, Joanna Lumley, Leo McKern, Geoffrey Palmer, James Robertson Justice, Prunella Scales, Peter Ustinov, Edmund Petheridge.

Television Characters: 'M' in *James Bond* (*Judi Dench*), Jean and Lionel Hardcastle in *As Time Goes By* (*Judi Dench and Geoffrey Palmer*), Miss Marple (*Joan Hickson*), Jerry Leadbetter in *The Good Life* (*Paul Eddington*), Sir Humphrey Appleby and Jim Hacker in *Yes, Minister* (*Nigel Hawthorne and Paul Eddington*).

Characters and Plays: Lady and Sir Robert Chiltern (*An Ideal Husband*), Major Barbara (*Major Barbara*), Henry Higgins and Eliza Doolittle (*Pygmalion*), Arthur and Grace Winslow (*The Winslow Boy*), Osborne and Raleigh (*Journey's End*).

Hear it: *Track 81.* 'Arthur the Rat'

The GROOVE

The rhythm has a distinct swing to it, created by strong distinctions between stressed and unstressed syllables. Let the weight and momentum swing to the Landing Point, then swing to the next, with any little syllables on the way becoming light and rapid.

The tune works on the vertical, with large leaps up and down to the Landing Points in the phrase. Really open up the distance between the notes and use the final cadences or inflections for dramatic or subtextual impact. Small changes in these can turn an apparently innocent remark into a cutting comment.

Embody It

Physical Actions: An exercise favoured by old elocution teachers was to use a chiffon scarf to swing through the phrase, a little like the actions used in rhythmic gymnastics. Try it. Swing the chiffon in front of you, like a conductor, using its heaviest point as the Landing Point of the phrase (for a fuller description of this exercise see pages 30-31). You can also explore the range by imagining you are playing scales on a piano or climbing up and down a ladder.

Laban Actions: Rapid Dabs with Glides on the Landing Points.

 See It:

DAB   GLIDE

 Hear It: Track 81. Listen for these qualities in *Arthur the Rat.*

 Feel It: This only really makes sense when you actually do it, so have a go. Swing a chiffon scarf or, if there's no chiffon to hand, a long piece of loo paper will do! Try using the actions of dabbing and gliding with your hands, or even to move around the room. And be sure to try climbing up and down the ladders of the tune!

Refine It

 Hear It: Track 81. Listen to the line, 'There was once a young rat named Arthur, who could never take the trouble to make up his mind' and sing the tune you hear.

 Feel It: Now combine the swinging chiffon scarf, the dabs and glides, and the rungs of a ladder with the new tune.

The FOUNDATIONS

The external face is kept elegant, relaxed and undisturbed, not revealing too much of the emotions that may lie beneath, while the inside workings of the tongue and soft palate are precise and efficient. It is the tongue that bears the responsibility for the clarity of the sound on the inside of the mouth, while the external muscles use as little muscular engagement as is necessary; no more, no less. The result is a certain delicacy, together with a muscular clarity.

Setting

Jaw and Cheeks: Loosely maintain a space between the back teeth and in the back of the mouth *at all times*. The jaw and cheeks have the job of maintaining the appropriate space in the mouth to allow the more precise work of the tongue to happen. There is no spreading in the cheeks at all, the face feels long and narrow.

Lips: Think of a slight pout, the pillows plumped, the top lip lifted slightly, no spreading *at all!* Think of the vowels as vertical and narrow rather than horizontal and wide.

Tongue: The tongue lies forward in the mouth, the tip resting against the bottom teeth. Here's how you can achieve the setting of the tongue; while keeping the tip behind the bottom teeth, allow the middle of the tongue to rise up and roll forward a little and then pant like a puppy! Then relax the mouth gently over this tongue position. The *tip* needs to be flexible enough to find the gum-ridge without the jaw having to close. The *back* must also be strong and flexible, able to shape those dark, low frequency vowels such as GOOSE and THOUGHT.

Soft Palate: The soft palate is a little raised, like holding it on the edge of a yawn. Imagine you have just eaten a piece of hot potato, but are too polite to spit it out!

Zone: 1-2

See It:

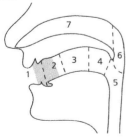

The sound aims for 'the tip of the tongue, the teeth and the lips', as the old articulation exercise goes. It can actually help to focus on a point *beyond* your mouth, where you might hold a candle to blow out, and aim your sound there, clearing any obstacle that may be in the way.

Tone

The resultant tone is bright with an underlying warmth, like a harp.

Hear It: Listen to the harp video and Traditional RP examples at www.howtodoaccents.com

Direction

See It:

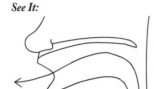

Forward on a wave, sending the sound to the listener.

Hesitation Sound

As a result of the Foundations described, the hesitation sound is a little further forward and raised from the neutral position...lift it forward and up from the midline, towards the gum-ridge. Sprinkle a little DRESS onto the sound.

Putting it all together

Begin by counting to ten, focusing on maintaining the setting, zone, tone and direction.

Hear It: *Track 82.*

Increase this to days of the week, and months of the year, before trying a piece of text.

Planet Non-Rhotic ————————————————

Remember, ALL Standard English Accents are Non-Rhotic! (see page 43).

Hear It: *Track 83.* You will hear linking 'Rs' (see page 45) in this variety:

    fear and horror   for a new home

...but probably not intrusive 'Rs' (see page 46)

Hear It: *Track 84.*

    the idea of (not idea r of)   they saw a young rat (not saw r a)

The BITE

Major Players

R L H NG TH

'R' : Tap it lightly on the gum-ridge between vowels, especially between the front vowels such as KIT, DRESS and TRAP, both within words and between words:

> very   marry   here I go

To do a tap, make a quick 'D' lightly on the gum-ridge between the vowels (see page 103).

Major Issues

'T' : Lift the tip of the tongue onto the gum-ridge, without any tension in the jaw at all, the teeth staying apart. It is a light, delicate tap, without a 'splash'.

> Do take Dotty and Ted a better bit of butter for their tea and toast.

WHICH v WITCH: distinguish words with 'WH' by adding a slight puff of air through the lips before the 'W', almost like 'hwat', 'hwere', etc. NB. Careful, don't overdo this, it is very gentle in this accent.

> what–watt   where–wear   why–Y   which–witch   whether–weather

'YOOs' : After *all* gum-ridge and dental consonants.

> Rather than be lewd, he presumed it was his duty to play a suitable tune with enthusiasm.

Try seeing the word either with a 'YOO' or with 'EE'-'OO' to help your mouth along.

> lyood / lee-ood   prezyoomed / prezee-oomed   dyooty / dee-ooty
> syootable /see-ootable   tyoon / tee-oon   enthyoosisam / enthee-oosiasm

Hear It: Track 85. Listen to these Major Players and Major Issues and have a go yourself.

All the other Major Players and Issues are the same as a New Standard English Accent.

The SHAPES

As a result of the Foundations and possibly the influence of Hanoverian German (see *The Frame*, page 137) the vowels at the front of the mouth move forward and up, while those at the back move further back.

Hear It: Track 86. The Kit List and practice sentences.

KIT: This set have a shape that is closer to being a short version of a FLEECE vowel. Sprinkle a little 'EE' onto it, keep the sound bright, focus it onto the philtrum (that's the bit above your top lip and under your nose), high and forward, and spread the sound across the gum-ridge.

The ship listed as busy women built a pretty bridge in the dim mid-winter.

DRESS: The DRESS vowel moves into the new KIT territory, so imagine you are *almost* saying DRISS! Use the puppy dog setting described in the Foundations to help with this shape.

In a sweat (swit), Jeff (Jiff) edged (idged) his head (hid) into the Thames (Tims) in an effort (iffort) to save his best (bist) friend (frind) from the treacherous (tricherous) bell (bill) of death (dith).

STRUT: The open vertical setting gives a little extra space to this shape. Sprinkle a tiny bit of 'AH' onto the sound.

The dull young monks rushed in a flood to hunt the buds of the lovely buttercup.

FOOT: The hump in the tongue is high and quite far back, which gives this a much 'darker', lower quality than the New Standard English Accent. Be sure to round and pout the lips forward as if around your little finger. To modern ears this will sound very close to a short GOOSE vowel.

The woman shouldn't put the full pudding onto the butcher's hook.

GOOSE: Maximise the full, deep 'owl-hoot' resonance with the back of the tongue high. Round and pout the lips, as if around a pencil. Use the *inner* muscle of the lip, and the thrust in the cheeks to push the lips forward while keeping them plump. Make a 'G' and then slightly release the tongue into the owl hoot to feel the back of the tongue in this raised position.

Two beautiful youths moved through a few smooth, juicy, rude grooves in feudal confusion.

FLEECE: This is almost as extreme as it can be. Keep it bright and sparkly by squeezing the hump in the tongue up the centre point of the gum-ridge, and fill up the resonance behind it.

The police had reason to believe that Peter, Keith and the anaemic Sheila could be in league to illegally deceive people.

NURSE: (No 'R'!) As with the hesitation sound, this vowel lifts slightly up from the midline, towards the gum-ridge and buzzes onto the top lip. Sprinkle a little DRESS onto the sound. There is absolutely NO lip-rounding. If anything, the lips feel a *tiny* bit spread.

Pearl urged Myrtle's attorney to rehearse a certain circus turn before the courteous worm turned.

TRAP: Imagine you are saying TREP, but be sure to open the jaw vertically, rather than using tight lips. Use the puppy dog setting described in the Foundations to help with this shape. This is one of the key changes in this accent!

The cat (ket) dashed (deshed) to catch (ketch) the ham (hem) that (thet) dangled (dengled) from the bag (beg).

BATH–PALM–START: (No 'R'!) This isn't that different in shape from a New Standard English Accent. It's an open vowel, with relaxed cheeks and lips, and an 'AH' quality. Keep the jaw open and relaxed, the vowel towards the back of the tongue, but not too plummy! Remember these sets merge in *all* Standard English Accents, so be sure to make them rhyme!

BATH: 'Francis the calf can't dance', laughed Sandra the giraffe, aghast, as the calf pranced disastrously.

PALM: Brahms' sonata kept father calm in the spa.

START: Sergeant Charles was the star of the party with his hearty aria.

LOT: Much like New Standard English Accent, the jaw is dropped open, while the cheeks are hollowed, and the lips rounded and pushing gently forward. There is a slight hump in the back of the tongue that shapes the sound. The resonance is at the back of the mouth and has a low quality. Keep it snappy, this is a short vowel. (NB. The words *was, because* and *of* are all in this set when they are stressed in a sentence!)

Tom honestly acknowledged how top-notch the swan was to dodge the yacht.

CLOTH: After the Second World War this set began to merge with LOT, but in older accents/speakers it merged with THOUGHT etc., especially before 'S', 'F' and voiceless 'TH'. The result is that during the 1940s, 1950s and 1960s some words hovered between the two sets!

Ross often frothed the coffee and washed the long sausages in Boston.

She lost the cross when it fell off the cloth.

THOUGHT–NORTH–FORCE: (No 'R'!) Again this is much like the New Standard English Accent shape. From the LOT shape (described above), close the lips a little, like drawing the purse string very slightly tighter, engage the 'thrust muscle' of the cheeks a little more, and then add the *length* that really makes this vowel (yes, even in the THOUGHT sound, in spite of the lack of 'R'!). Remember these sets merge in *all* Standard English Accents, so be sure to make them rhyme!

> **THOUGHT:** Paul applauded all the naughty daughters who yawned when taught with chalk and talk.

> **NORTH:** George cavorted with Thor to fortify his short torso for the war in York.

> **FORCE:** 'Of course I adore Nora', roared the porter through the door to the four divorced boarders.

FACE: This becomes a very tiny slide from the raised DRESS vowel to the raised KIT vowel, making it almost Extreme Vowel 2 (as in the French vowel in *du thé*). Thinking of it as a FLEECE vowel can help the tongue into position.

> April felt faint as she campaigned to rein in the wasteful ladies to change their ways and obey.

GOAT–*GOAL*: Start from the slightly forward hesitation sound, with a little preparatory lip-rounding, and slide to the FOOT vowel. A **key feature** of upper-class varieties is the lack of any L Effect on this vowel, so be sure to use **exactly** the same sound and shape in the GOAL words, too (shown in **bold**). This can take practice!

> Joan coaxed her beau, Owen, to grow **bold**er, though she loathed over-**controlling soldiers.**

PRICE: Push this slide a little further forward in the mouth than in a New Standard English Accent to keep it bright and sparkly! Begin the slide from the TRAP and slide only as far as KIT. Put a little more weight in the first half of the slide. Remember, this is your personal pronoun, 'I', so be sure to anchor this sound to your centre and connect it to your sense of self.

> Friday is the right night to arrive by bicycle in Cyprus to buy a fine eiderdown.

CHOICE: Unlike the New Standard English Accent, this starts from the LOT shape (as described above), not a THOUGHT shape, and only slides to KIT. Again, put a little more weight in the first half of the slide.

> The boy employed a joist to hoist the moist oysters into the boiling oil.

MOUTH: Start from BATH and slide to FOOT. This gives slide a much richer, lower resonant quality than is heard in more modern accents.

TRAD RP

> The loud crowd from south of the county wanted to oust the clown out of town, but they were all mouth.

NEAR: (No 'R'!) Be sure to have a slide in this shape. For this to be possible, start from the raised KIT so you can slide to the commA vowel.

> Maria was sincere in her weird career, but feared the fierce bearded cashier.

SQUARE: (No 'R'!) Again, be sure to have a slide! This can only happen if you start from the raised DRESS shape, giving yourself plenty of room to slide to the commA vowel.

> Where the pears are scarce, the bears share theirs fairly.

TOUR: (No 'R'!) In older accents this was a set that didn't merge with NURSE or THOUGHT, but was a set of its own. Words in this set had a lovely little slide from the FOOT vowel to the commA vowel. Like blowing a kiss.

> Muriel assured the poor tourists that the insurance was sure to cover Europe.

NB. Paw–Pour–Poor: words from the NORTH and FORCE sets where the vowel is in the final position (though spelled with an 'R') such as WAR, MORE, THOR, may be distinguished by adding a slide to a final schwa. This makes the words PAW and POUR distinct in this accent and creates a three-way split with POOR!

Environmental Issues

Vowel Clusters and Collisions:

Smoothing: Gentle.

A general feature of all upper-class accents is the use of smoothing to a greater or lesser degree.

'Smoothing' refers to the 'smoothing out' of the vowel slides that happen when two or more vowels from the Kit List meet.

For example, in the word 'science', the PRICE vowel meets the schwa, making a slide through three shapes: 'A–I–UH'. To smooth this slide out, remove the middle shape completely, losing any feeling of 'Y' from the tongue, leaving you with 'SA-UNCE' or even 'SAHNCE'.

This also happens when words meet... Try saying the following, losing any feeling of 'W' or 'Y' between these words:

> GO OUT   DO IT   PLAY ON

For a traditional sound that is not too extreme, use only *gentle* smoothing:

Hear It: Track 87.

fire ('fa-i-uh') smoothes to 'fa-uh'

power ('pa-oo-uh') smoothes to 'pa-uh'

throwing ('thruh-oo-ing') smoothes to 'thruh-ing'

Vowels followed by 'ER' and 'ING' are the most common to be subject to smoothing:

player   lawyer   mower   higher   tower

fleeing   drawing   doing   playing   bowing   lying   annoying

GOING: The very forward position of the tongue at the start of the GOAT vowel means that when it is said quickly, without any stress, there is not even a hint of a 'W' or lip-rounding in the middle of this word. 'Going home' = 'gung hum' or 'geng hem'.

Hear It: Track 88.

We were **going** to a party in **Lower** Loxeley, bowling along with considerable **power, trying** to get to it on time.'Who are we **seeing** there?' I asked.'Oh, some very **annoying** people', he answered. 'There'll be **Howard**, the incessant card **player**, and my Aunt the **lawye**r, **doing** her usual party piece. They'll be in the **drawing** room, gathered around the **fire, chewing** the fat, **playin**g "who is the smartest", **allowing** no one else to get a word in. How **tire**some!'

Vowel Reductions: The little sounds with a big impact!

When a syllable has no weight or stress in it, the vowel is 'reduced' to something shorter and less open than it would be otherwise. How many syllables are reduced, and which vowel is used can make a huge difference to the quality of the accent.

Older upper-class accents had a strong tendency to *minimise* the number of stressed syllables in a word, often stressing only one syllable in multisyllabic words. This means that vowels are being reduced left, right and centre!

Here are some key words that are stressed differently as a result:

Hear It: Track 89.

necessary = NEsusry   circumstances = CIRcumstunsiz

momentarily = MOmuntruly

finance = fiNANCE   portrait = PORtrut

This feature extends to *all* 'ORY', 'ARY', 'ONY' etc. endings:

inventory = INvuntry   library = LIbry   alimony = ALimuny

happY: This little ending is a short KIT vowel in older upper-class accents.
Hear It: Track 90.

Billy and Mary were happy to see the movie, 'When Harry Met Sally'. Billy had a coffee, and Mary bought a pastry.

FLEECE and **GOOSE** vowels shorten to KIT and FOOT final unstressed positions:

He loves me   We shall be   She was, was she?   Would you   The igloo

commA–lettER: Use a slightly forward schwa. Sprinkle a little dress onto it.
Hear It: Track 91.

gather   writer   anger   India   Diana   yoga

privATE word endings:

These little endings have changed over time. In contemporary accents they have a commA vowel, but in older varieties they all had the KIT vowel:

Hear It: Track 92.

toilet (bracelet, pamphlet, etc.) = TOI–*lit*

private (climate, etc.) = PRI–*vit*

problem (system, Blenheim, etc.) = PROB–*lim*

kindness (countless, business, etc.) = KIND–*niss*

horsES word endings:

The following little endings also use a KIT vowel in *all* varieties of Standard English, so watch out if your accent uses a commA vowel!

horses (foxes, daises, marries, etc.) = HOR–*siz*

wasted (landed, excited, etc.) = WAS–*tid*

longest (biggest, forest, etc.) = LONG–*gist*

active (massive, etc.) = AC–*tiv*

pocket (biscuit, planet, etc.) = PO–*kit*

college (sausage, baggage, package, etc.) = CO–*lidge*

surface (office) = SUR–*fiss*

Finally, for our North American friends with good intentions, we must mention and draw attention to the convention of...

TION endings: It is crucial that these have a tiny commA vowel, and not a nasalised KIT vowel in them. This tiny detail can be a real giveaway! For example:

Hear It: Track 93.

attention = attensh**un**, not attensh**in**

mission = missh**un**, not missh**in**

station = staysh**un**, not staysh**in**

And that's Traditional RP! Of course it has some similarities to our current New Standard English Accent, but it will always have that extra something that makes it sound old-fashioned or just plain posh.

So what other kinds are there? Well, in truth there are probably as many varieties as there are people, in that every speaker has his or her idiosyncrasies, however in the next few chapters we will describe some of the most useful identifiable varieties, all of them class-based accents. Use them individually, or mix and match to create your own unique character.

IMPERIAL LORDS AND LADIES

The FRAME

This is the archetypal accent of the older upper classes. It speaks of old money, strong lineage, eccentric upbringings and privilege. The lifestyle applies little pressure in terms of either physical space or time. There is a sense of entitlement that comes from family history, together with an equally strong sense of responsibility for continuity into future generations. They espouse the values of tradition, aesthetics, good manners and propriety. There are strong connections to the country, to landscapes and the seasons, art and architecture, and an unromantic, practical connection to nature. The biblical quotation, they 'have dominion', describes them well. In this world there is a place for everyone, and everyone in his place. It is the accent that provided the template for much of the Old Stage Standard accent as heard in people such as Mrs Patrick Campbell and Herbert Beerbohm Tree (see *Nod to the Old Wave*, page 149).

The focus is on vowels, more than consonants. Consonants, though clearly made, are also relatively soft, unlike the sharp strength in the consonants of the Military variety. In this accent there is no need to bark orders! There is no hurry, just as in the lifestyle, everything has a rhythm, a time and a place. There is a sense of continuity.

People: Mrs. Patrick Campbell, Harold Macmillan, Jeremy Thorpe, Iris Murdoch, Margaret Rutherford, Margaret Tyzack, Robert Hardy, Donald Sinden, Vita Sackville-West, Virginia Woolf, Peregrine Worsthorne.

Television/Film Characters: Lady Southwold and Lady Marjorie (*Upstairs Downstairs*), Lord Brideshead (*Brideshead Revisited*), Lady Elms (BBC *The Hour*), Countess of Trentham (*Gosford Park*), Violet Crawley (*Downton Abbey*), Lord Stockbridge (*Gosford Park*).

Characters and Plays: Lady Markby and the Earl of Caversham (*An Ideal Husband*), Sir Robert Morton (*The Winslow Boy*), Lord Undershaft and Lady Britomart (*Major Barbara*), Duchess of Berwick (*Lady Windermere's Fan*), Lady Bracknell (*The Importance of Being Earnest*), Sir Johnstone Kentley (*Rope*). Indeed the majority of Coward, Bernard Shaw, Rattigan, Wilde, Harley Granville-Barker and the like will have characters suitable for this variety.

Hear it: *Track 94.* 'Arthur the Rat'.

The GROOVE

The rhythm is slow, pedantic and measured, with sudden bursts of enthusiasm.

The tune is firmly major in quality, using large major cadences, and an easy use of range, with a factual, effortlessly confident stride to it.

Embody it

Physical Actions: Striding upstream in hip-waders. A slow canter with occasional jumps.

Laban Actions: Generally Press with Dab or Punch when excited, or drifting into a Float as the thoughts become more vague.

 See It:

PRESS

 Hear It: Track 94. Listen for these qualities.

 Feel It: This only really makes sense when you actually do it, so have a go! Try striding, wading, or cantering around the room or with your arms as you speak.

Refine It

 Hear It: Track 94. Listen to the line, 'There was once a young rat named Arthur, who could never take the trouble to make up his mind' and sing the tune you hear.

Feel it: Now combine the words with the physical actions with the new tune.

The FOUNDATIONS

The body is robust without being rigid, well-nourished and extremely well poised and balanced, not least as a result of good horsemanship! Their presence expands into the space and occupies full height with a sense of ease. The external face is kept elegant, relaxed and undisturbed, as if sitting for a portrait, with the occasional expressive arch of an eyebrow. Inside the mouth the movements of the tongue and soft palate are precise and efficient. It is the tongue that bears the responsibility for the clarity of the sound while the external muscles use as little engagement as possible; just the most delicate use of the thrust muscle through the cheeks to push the lips forward for the rounded vowels. The phrase '*pas devant les domestiques*' or 'not in front of the servants', comes to mind.

Setting

Jaw and Cheeks: Loosely maintain a space between the back teeth and in the back of the mouth at all times, as if the face is hanging off the cheekbones like a sleepy horse! Use the thrust muscle through the line of the cheekbone to push the lips forward for the rounded vowels.

Lips: Are used as little as is necessary, no more, but no less! They are never tight, nor do they disturb the overall portrait.

Tongue: The tongue lies forward in the mouth, the tip resting against the bottom teeth. The tip has to be flexible enough to find the gum-ridge without disturbing the looseness of the jaw, while the back is also strong and flexible, able to shape the rich, dark vowels at the back of the mouth without overly relying on the lips.

Soft Palate: The soft palate is a little raised, like holding it on the edge of a yawn.

Zone: 4-5
See It:

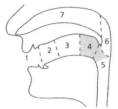

The sound collects behind the muscular back of the tongue, at the top of the throat, and in a pocket between the molars.

Tone
The resultant tone is deep, 'plummy', like a classical double bass with the occasional dinner gong.

Direction
See It:

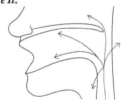

Fill yourself with sound and make it multi-directional.

Hesitation Sound
The loose jaw, raised soft palate and forward-rolled tongue make the relaxed sound of the mouth a vowel just slightly forward from the neutral commA vowel or schwa.

Putting it all together

Begin by counting to ten, focusing on maintaining the setting, zone, tone and direction.

Hear It: Track 95. Hesitation sound followed by numbers.

Increase this to days of the week, and months of the year, before trying a piece of text.

Planet Non-Rhotic

Remember, ALL Standard English Accents are Non-Rhotic! (see page 43).
You will hear linking 'Rs' (see page 45) in this variety:

Hear It: *Track 96.*

> search fora new home   good food forus all

and possibly a very light, gentle intrusive 'R' after a commA vowel, but definitely
not after a THOUGHT vowel:

Hear It: *Track 97.*

> idea rof   they saw a young rat   (not saw ra)

The BITE

Major Players

R Lн NGтн

'R': Taps lightly on the gum-ridge between vowels, especially between the
front vowels such as KIT, DRESS and TRAP, both within words and between
words:

> very   marry   here I go

To tap, make a quick 'D' lightly on the gum-ridge between vowels.

It may also tap in clusters with other consonants for emphasis or dramatic
effect:

> bring   freddy   great   cry

'L': In some speakers the 'L' before a consonant (field) or in a final position
(hill) is surprisingly light. This may well be another remnant of the Hanoverian
ancestry coming through.

> little   hills   fields

Hear It: *Track 98.*

Hear It: To hear these features, listen to Vita Sackville-West and Jennifer
Paterson (the dark-haired half of the *Two Fat Ladies*). Find examples at
www.howtodoaccents.com.

'NG': Although usually the same as in a NSEA, in extremely old versions of
this accent there was a dropped 'N' variant on 'ING' verb endings. You may well
have heard or seen the phrase *huntin', shootin' and fishin'* used by aristocratic
characters. This feature goes back to Middle English when it was a perfectly

correct way of distinguishing the verb from the gerund. Though the distinction died out from Standard English, it persisted in the extremes of the upper classes right up until the end of the 19th century and can often be seen in the words of characters in Restoration plays.

Major Issues

'T': Lift the tip of the tongue onto the gum-ridge, without any tension in the jaw at all, the teeth staying apart. It is a light, delicate tap without any 'splash'.

Do take Dotty and Ted a better bit of butter for their tea and toast.

'P' 'T' 'K': These can all be noticeably un-aspirated. This simply means the contact is held and then cleanly released, with no 'splash' at all! This is similar in quality to other accents of the Empire such as Indian and South African.

Poppy, Tommy and Colin acted in a terrible comedy play.

Hear it: Vita Sackville-West is a perfect example of this feature in action at www.howtodoaccents.com.

WHICH v WITCH: Distinguish words beginning with 'WH' by adding a slight puff of air through the lips before the 'W', almost like 'hwat', 'hwere', etc. NB. Careful, don't overdo this, it is only gentle in this accent.

what–watt   where–wear   why–Y   which–witch
whether–weather

'YOOs': After *all* gum-ridge and dental consonants.

Rather than be lewd, he presumed it was his duty to play a suitable tune with enthusiasm.

Try seeing the word either with a 'YOO' or with 'EE-OO' to help your mouth along.

lyood / lee-ood   prezyoomed / prezee-oomed   dyooty / dee-ooty
syootable / see-ootable   tyoon / tee-oon
enthyoosisam / enthee-oosiasm

Hear It: Track 99. Listen to these Major Issues and have a go yourself.

All the other Major Players and Issues are the same as a New Standard English Accent.

The SHAPES

Because of the nature of the Foundations (and possibly the influence of Hanoverian German!) the vowels at the front of the mouth move forward and up, those in the middle are a little more open and those at the back move even further back. With the 'round' vowels be sure not to overuse the lips or tense the jaw. It is the height of the tongue at the back that creates the low resonance.

Hear It: Track 100. 'The Kit List'.

KIT: This set has a shape that is closer to being a short version of a FLEECE vowel. Sprinkle a little 'EE' onto it, keep the sound bright, focus it onto the philtrum, high and forward, and spread the sound across the gum-ridge.

> The ship listed as busy women built a pretty bridge in the dim mid-winter.

DRESS: The DRESS vowel has moved into the KIT territory, so imagine you are *almost* saying DRISS!

> In a sweat (swit), Jeff (Jiff) edged (idged) his head (hid) into the Thames (Tims) in an effort (iffort) to save his best (bist) friend (frind) from the treacherous (tricherous) bell (bill) of death (dith).

STRUT: The open vertical setting gives a little extra space to this shape.

> The dull young monks rushed in a flood to hunt the buds of the lovely buttercup.

FOOT: The hump in the tongue is high and quite far back which gives this a 'darker', lower quality than the New Standard English Accent. Be sure to round and pout the lips forward. To modern ears this will sound very close to a short GOOSE vowel.

> The woman shouldn't put the full pudding onto the butcher's hook.

GOOSE: Maximise the full, deep 'owl-hoot' resonance with the back of the tongue high (make a 'G' and then slightly release the tongue to feel the back of the tongue in its raised position). Round and pout the lips forward very gently. It is the tongue that does the bulk of the work!

> Two beautiful youths moved through a few smooth, juicy, rude grooves in feudal confusion.

FLEECE: This is almost as extreme as it can be. Keep it bright and sparkly by squeezing the hump in the tongue up the centre point of the gum-ridge, and fill up the resonance behind it.

> The police had reason to believe that Peter, Keith and the anaemic Sheila could be in league to illegally deceive people.

NURSE: (No 'R'!) As with the hesitation sound, this vowel lifts slightly up from the midline, towards the gum-ridge and buzzes onto the top lip. Sprinkle a little DRESS onto the sound. There is absolutely NO lip-rounding. Let the lips relax completely.

> Pearl urged Myrtle's attorney to rehearse a certain circus turn before the courteous worm turned.

TRAP: Imagine you are saying TREP, but be sure to open the jaw vertically, rather than using tight lips. This is one of the most noticeable changes in this accent.

> The cat (ket) dashed (deshed) to catch (ketch) the ham (hem) that (thet) dangled (dengled) from the bag (beg).

BATH–PALM–START: (No 'R'!) Let the 'AH' vowel drop back in the mouth, as if it might fall down your throat! This gives it a more 'plummy' quality. And remember, these sets merge in *all* Standard English Accents, so be sure to make them rhyme!

> **BATH:** 'Francis the calf can't dance', laughed Sandra the giraffe, aghast, as the calf pranced disastrously.
> **PALM:** Brahms' sonata kept father calm in the spa.
> **START:** Sergeant Charles was the star of the party with his hearty aria.

LOT–CLOTH: Although it sounds rounded, the lips, in fact, do very little. It is the raising and tensing of the back of the tongue that achieves the low resonance. (NB. The words *was, because* and *of* are all in this set when they are stressed in a sentence!)

> **LOT:** Tom honestly acknowledged how top-notch the swan was to dodge the yacht.
> **CLOTH:** Ross often frothed the coffee and washed the long sausages in Boston.

(CLOTH) THOUGHT–NORTH–FORCE: (No 'R'!) Get the length in the THOUGHT sound, in spite of the lack of 'R'. Engage the 'thrust muscle' of the cheeks a little, but not using any inner lip tension.

In older upper-class accents (and older London accents too!) many words from the CLOTH set merged with the THOUGHT set, especially before the sounds 'S', 'F' and voiceless 'TH'.

> She lost the cross when it fell off the cloth

A gorgeously archaic feature, specific to this variety, is that some words with 'AU' spellings may jump ship and merge instead with the BATH set, i.e.

> Laundry = *LAHndry*   Launch = *LAHnch*   Haunches = *HAHnches*

IMP L&L

THOUGHT: Paul applauded all the naughty daughters who yawned when taught with chalk and talk.

NORTH: George cavorted with Thor to fortify his short torso for the war in York.

FORCE: 'Of course I adore Nora', roared the porter through the door to the four divorced boarders.

FACE: This becomes a very tiny slide from the raised DRESS vowel to the raised KIT vowel. You could almost think of it as a FLEECE vowel to help the tongue into position.

April felt faint as she campaigned to rein in the wasteful ladies to change their ways and obey.

GOAT–*GOAL*: Start from the slightly forward schwa, with a little preparatory lip-rounding, and slide to the FOOT vowel. No need to round the lips though! Be sure to use exactly the same sound and shape in the GOAL words, too (shown in **bold**):

Joan coaxed her beau, Owen, to grow **bold**er, though she loathed over-**controlling soldiers.**

PRICE: Start from a slightly forward STRUT with a sprinkle of TRAP on it. Slide to KIT, but only half-heartedly! Remember, this is your personal pronoun, 'I', so be sure to anchor this sound to your centre and connect it to your sense of self.

Friday is the right night to arrive by bicycle in Cyprus to buy a fine eiderdown.

CHOICE: Unlike in a New Standard English Accent, this starts from the LOT shape (as described above), not a THOUGHT shape, and only slides to KIT, again somewhat half-heartedly. Put the weight into the first half of the slide.

The boy employed a joist to hoist the moist oysters into the boiling oil.

MOUTH: Start from the BATH described above, right at the back of the tongue and slide to FOOT. This gives slide a much more 'plummy', low resonant quality than is heard in more modern accents.

The loud crowd from south of the county wanted to oust the clown out of town, but they were all mouth.

NEAR: You can make this almost the same as SQUARE, with the tongue not quite making it to the KIT position to start the slide. This makes the words *Really* and *Rarely* difficult to tell apart!

Maria was sincere in her weird career, but feared the fierce bearded cashier.

SQUARE: Start from the raised DRESS and slide to the schwa.

Where the pears are scarce, the bears share theirs fairly.

TOUR: (NO 'R'!) In older accents this was a set that didn't merge with NURSE or THOUGHT, but was a set of its own. Words in this set had a lovely little slide from the foot vowel to the schwa. Like blowing a kiss.

Muriel assured the poor tourists that the insurance was sure to cover Europe.

NB. See the note on page 145 regarding the PAW–POUR–POOR split!

Environmental Issues

Vowel Clusters and Collisions:

Smoothing: Extreme!

A general feature of all upper-class accents is the use of smoothing to a greater or lesser degree.

'Smoothing' refers to the 'smoothing out' of the vowel slides that happen when two or more vowels from the Kit List meet.

For example, in the word 'science', the PRICE vowel meets the schwa, making a slide through three shapes: 'A–I–UH'. To smooth this slide out, remove the middle shape completely, losing any feeling of 'Y' from the tongue, leaving you with 'SA–UNCE' or even 'SAHNCE'.

This also happens when words meet… Try saying the following, losing any feeling of 'W' or 'Y' between these words:

GO OUT   DO IT   PLAY ON

This variety uses *extreme* smoothing:

Hear It: Track 101.

fire ('fa-i-uh') smoothes to 'fah'

power ('pa-oo-uh') smoothes to 'pah'

throwing ('thruh-oo-ing') smoothes to 'thruhng'

Vowels followed by 'ER' and 'ING' are the most common to be subject to smoothing:

player   lawyer   mower   higher   tower

fleeing   drawing   doing   playing   bowing   lying   annoying

GOING. The very forward position of the tongue at the start of the GOAT vowel means that when it is said quickly, without any stress, there is not even a hint of a 'W' or lip-rounding in the middle of this word. 'Going home' = 'gung hum' or 'geng hem'.

Hear It: *Track 102.*

> We were **going** to a party in **Lower** Loxeley, bowling along with considerable **power, trying** to get to it on time. 'Who are we **seeing** there?' I asked. 'Oh, some very **annoying** people', he answered. 'There'll be **Howard**, the incessant card **player**, and my Aunt the **lawye**r, **doing** her usual party piece. They'll be in the **drawing** room, gathered around the **fire, chewing** the fat, **playin**g "who is the smartest", **allowing** no one else to get a word in. How **tire**some!'

Vowel Reductions: The little sounds with a big impact!

When a syllable has no weight, or stress in it, the vowel is 'reduced' to something shorter and less open than it would be otherwise. How many syllables are reduced, and which vowel is used, can make a huge difference to the quality of the accent.

Older upper-class accents had a strong tendency to *minimise* the number of stressed syllables in a word, often stressing only one syllable in multisyllabic words. This means that vowels are being reduced left, right and centre!

Hear It: *Track 89.*

Here are some key words that are stressed differently as a result:

necessary = NEsusry   circumstances = CIRcumstunsiz

momentarily = MOmuntruly

finance = fiNANCE   portrait = PORtrut

This feature extends to *all* 'ORY', 'ARY', 'ONY', etc. endings.

inventory = INvuntry   library = LIbry   alimony = ALimuny

happY: This little ending is a short KIT vowel in older upper-class accents (but remember the action of PRESS in the Groove? Although this is a KIT vowel, it can lengthen a little as a result!):

Hear It: *Track 90.*

> Billy and Mary were happy to see the movie, 'When Harry Met Sally'. Billy had a coffee, and Mary bought a pastry.

FLEECE and GOOSE: these become KIT and FOOT in final unstressed positions.

He loves m**e**.   We shall b**e**.   Sh**e** was, was sh**e**?   Would y**ou**   The igl**oo**

commA–lettER: These endings may be a little more open and lengthened in comparison with Traditional RP:

Hear It: Track 91.

gather   writer   anger   India   Diana   yoga

privATE word endings:

These little endings have changed over time. In contemporary accents they have a commA vowel, but in older varieties they all had the KIT vowel:

Hear It: Track 92.

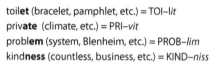

toil**et** (bracelet, pamphlet, etc.) = TOI–l*it*
priv**ate** (climate, etc.) = PRI–*vit*
probl**em** (system, Blenheim, etc.) = PROB–*lim*
kind**ness** (countless, business, etc.) = KIND–*niss*

horsES word endings:

The following little endings also use a KIT vowel in *all* varieties of Standard English, so watch out if your accent uses a commA vowel!

hors**es** (foxes, daises, marries, etc.) = HOR–*siz*
wast**ed** (landed, excited, etc.) = WAS–*tid*
long**est** (biggest, forest, etc.) = LONG–*gist*
act**ive** (massive, etc.) = AC–*tiv*
pock**et** (biscuit, planet) = PO–*kit*
coll**ege** (sausage, baggage, package, etc.) = CO–*lidge*
surf**ace** (office) = SUR–*fiss*

Finally, for our North American friends with good intentions, we must mention and draw attention to the convention of...

TION endings: It is crucial that these have a tiny commA vowel, and not a nasalised KIT vowel in them. This tiny detail can be a real giveaway! For example:

Hear It: Track 93.

attention = *attenshun,* not *attenshin*
mission = *misshun,* not *misshin*
station = *stayshun,* not *stayshin*

MILITARY, MATRONS AND THE LANDED GENTRY

The FRAME

Often an off-shoot of the Imperial Lords and Ladies, these are the unromantic 'stuff and nonsense' brigade. They have a practical, pragmatic view of the world and are not afraid of taking charge. Although some may find their manner bossy, they are simply manifesting the skills necessary to manage horses, children or a regiment. They value tradition, order, discipline, and a practical good common-sense approach to life. They love the old-school country pursuits just as much as the Imperial Lords and Ladies, and are often more at home with animals than people.

People: Margaret Rutherford, Baroness Mary Warnock, Barbara Woodhouse, Clarissa Dickson Wright (*Two Fat Ladies*, the blonde one!), Arthur Lowe, Prince Charles, General the Lord Guthrie, General Mike Jackson, Princess Anne, Anne Leslie.

Television/Film/Radio Characters: *French and Saunders*, 'Two Ladies'. 'No 1' (Stephen Murray) in *The Navy Lark* (BBC Radio series), Captain Mainwaring (Arthur Lowe) in *Dad's Army*, and Captain Ashwood (Michael Knowles) and Lieutenant-Colonel Charles Reynolds (Donald Hewlett) in *It Ain't Half Hot Mum*, Colonel Blimp (*The Life and Death of Colonel Blimp*), Rowley Birkin QC (*The Fast Show*).

Characters and Plays: Colonel Pickering (*Pygmalion*), Admiral Boom (*Mary Poppins*), The Captains and Lieutenants (*Our Country's Good*), Colonel Redfern (*Look back In Anger*), Colonel Von Mohl (*A Patriot For Me*), General Haig and Sir John French (*Oh! What A lovely War*), Lt Colonel Barrow and Major Scott (*Tunes of Glory*), The Colonel (*Journey's End*), Mrs. Rafi (*The Sea*), Nora (*Alphabetical Order*), Miss Marple (all *Miss Marple Murder Mysteries*), Rebecca Huntley-Pike (*A Chorus of Disapproval*), Lady Gay Spanker (*London Assurance*).

Hear it: Track 103. 'Arthur the Rat'.

The GROOVE

The rhythm is punchy, strident, with sudden barks of sound.

The tune, while still operating on the vertical, may be somewhat flatter than Traditional RP, particularly in the men, as anything more might be considered unnecessarily sentimental! Occasional shots up into falsetto may be used to grab attention, or to express astonishment or exasperation, before dropping back down to the flat lands of fact. There is a major quality to the music and a tendency to use 'matter of fact' intonation patterns.

Embody It

Physical Actions: Following a bird's flight, then shooting it. Fencing with thrusts and parries. Chopping up meat with a heavy cleaver.

Laban Actions: Punch and Dab.

See it:

      PUNCH   DAB

Hear it: *Track 103.* Listen for these qualities.

Feel It: This only really makes sense when you actually do it, so have a go. Imagine you are punching and dabbing, chopping meat or following birds with a shot gun, and shooting them on the keywords to get the Groove into your body.

Refine It

Hear It: *Track 103.* Listen to the line, 'There was once a young rat named Arthur, who could never take the trouble to make up his mind' and sing the tune you hear.

Feel it: Now combine the words with the physical actions and the tune.

The FOUNDATIONS

The head is held straight on the spine, the eye contact either completely absent or very direct. The spine is strong and the stride solid and confident. Think sturdy boots and military footwear.

Setting

Jaw and Cheeks: A little held, with a sense of 'bite' in the jaw muscle. Try holding a pencil width-ways in your mouth, between your teeth while you speak, it really helps!

Lips: Taut. The top lip is especially held (stiff upper lip) with the bottom lip doing a little more of the work. The lips tend to stay flat and horizontal rather than rounding.

Tongue: The root of the tongue holds a little tension, while the back and tip exchange shapes dramatically in a relatively small space. The tongue tip is flatter and wider than in Traditional RP.

Soft Palate: Tight with a tendency to collect the sound and also direct it into the nose. This really affects the tone.

Zone

See It:

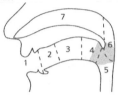

On the meeting point of 4-5-6. Access to points on the compass.

Tone

Strident and sharp like a bugle or an English horn with the weight of a tuba beneath it.

Direction

See It:

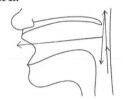

Shoots up and down at the back and then straight out to hit the target.

Hesitation sound

As a result of all the above, the relaxed sound of the mouth is close to a STRUT shape, a little wide and squashed, with a brassy tone.

Putting it all together

Begin by counting to ten, focusing on maintaining the setting, zone, tone and direction.

Hear It: *Track 104.* Hesitation sound followed by numbers.

Increase this to days of the week, and months of the year, before trying a piece of text.

Planet Non-Rhotic ─────────────────

Remember, ALL Standard English Accents are Non-Rhotic! (see page 43).

Hear It: *Track 105.*

You will hear linking 'Rs' (see page 45) in this variety:

> fearand horror   search fora new home
> thereis room and good food forus all   underit they saw

...and even intrusive 'Rs' after the schwa (see page 46):

idea of = idea rof

...though less likely after the THOUGHT vowel:

they saw a young rat (not saw r a)

The BITE

Major Players

R L H NG TH

'R': The 'R' may be rather weak, where the tongue hardly bends at all, or else it may tap for emphasis or in rapid speech. It is occasionally dropped completely in a word such as 'very' making it sound like 'vay'.

To tap, make a quick 'D' lightly on the gum-ridge between vowels, especially between the front vowels such as KIT, DRESS and TRAP, both within words and between words:

very   marry   here I go

Major Issues

'P', 'T', 'K': these voiceless plosives are often held, or suspended, on stressed syllables, before they explode into the remaining syllables, giving quite a gunshot feeling. Hold the consonant and then release.

PartiC-ularly   SimP-ly   ForT-unately

'T' and 'K': May also be accompanied, or even replaced by, a Glottal Stop between words:

rat named   like to go

get back   football   back drop

WHICH v WITCH: Unlike Traditional RP, this accent is unlikely to bother with these little distinctions, far too much fuss! The following examples therefore become identical pairs, as they are in a New Standard English Accent.

what–watt   where–wear   why–Y

which–witch   whether–weather

'YOOs': May be dropped after 'S' and crunched after 'T'.

Rather than be lewd, he presumed it was his duty to play a suitable tune with enthusiasm.

Try seeing the word either with a 'YOO' or with 'EE–OO' to help your mouth along:

lyood / lee-ood   prezyoomed / prezee-oomed
dyooty / dee-ooty   syootable / see-ootable
tyoon / tee-oon   enthyoosiasm / enthee-oosiasm

Crunching:

The tightness of the space can lead to crunching in some consonant collisions.

'DY': *Did you do your duty?* (The 'DY' crunches to 'J', as in Judge)
'TY': *I'll pass that tuna over to you.* (The 'TY' crunches to 'CH')
'DR': *I had a dream about druids.* (The 'DR' crunches to 'JR')
'TR': *The train ran out of petrol.* (The 'TR' crunches to 'CHR')

Hear It: Track 106. Listen to these Major Players and the Major Issues and have a go yourself.

All the other Major Players and Issues are the same as a New Standard English Accent.

The SHAPES

The Foundations and Groove make all the difference to this variety, giving all these vowel shapes a particular resonance and thrust from the abdomen.

Hear It: Track 107. 'The Kit List'.

KIT: Shoot it onto the gum-ridge.

The ship listed as busy women built a pretty bridge in the dim mid-winter.

DRESS: Close to a New Standard English Accent in position.

In a sweat, Jeff edged his head into the Thames in an effort to save his best friend from the treacherous bell of death.

STRUT: This is a little less open and wider than Traditional RP. Give it a TRAP-like quality.

The dull young monks rushed in a flood to hunt the buds of the lovely buttercup.

FOOT: Not as completely far back as Traditional RP, it is much more similar to NSEA, moving towards the middle of the mouth, with reluctant, somewhat flattened lip-rounding.

The woman shouldn't put the full pudding onto the butcher's hook.

GOOSE: As with FOOT, this lacks some of the beautiful owl resonance of Traditional RP, though when compared with the New Wave (see page 201), it is still considerably far back. Again the lips have reluctant, flattened rounding.

Two beautiful youths moved through a few smooth, juicy, rude grooves in feudal confusion.

FLEECE: Very tight, and often quite sudden in nature, shoot the sound onto the gum-ridge!

The police had reason to believe that Peter, Keith and the anaemic Sheila could be in league to illegally deceive people.

NURSE: (No 'R') As with the hesitation sound, this is close to a STRUT shape, a little wide and squashed, with a brassy tone.

Pearl urged Myrtle's attorney to rehearse a certain circus turn before the courteous worm turned.

TRAP: This is a variety that spans many generations. In older versions (born before circa 1960) you can use a vowel with a TREP quality as with Imperial Lords and Ladies. As the sound becomes more modern, the vowel opens and lowers towards the NSEA shape.

The cat (ket) dashed (deshed) to catch (ketch) the ham (hem) that (thet) dangled (dengled) from the bag (beg).

BATH–PALM–START: (No 'R'!) Further back than Traditional RP, this shape falls right to the back of the tongue and almost down the throat, where it is squashed by the back of the tongue and the soft palate. Remember these sets merge in *all* Standard English Accents, so be sure to make them rhyme!

BATH: 'Francis the calf can't dance', laughed Sandra the giraffe, aghast, as the calf pranced disastrously.

PALM: Brahms' sonata kept father calm in the spa.

START: Sergeant Charles was the star of the party with his hearty aria.

LOT–CLOTH: Make the tongue do the work. The back raises and tenses. Keep it nice and snappy with less attention on the lips. (NB. As with the Imperial Lords and Ladies *some* CLOTH words *may* merge with the THOUGHT set. The most likely contenders are single syllable words where the vowel is followed by 'F', 'TH' and 'S' such as *off, cloth* and *cost.*)

LOT: Tom honestly acknowledged how top-notch the swan was to dodge the yacht.

CLOTH: Ross often frothed the coffee and washed the long sausages in Boston.

MM&LG

THOUGHT–NORTH–FORCE: (No 'R'!) This shape practically vanishes down the back of the neck! Feel the back of the tongue and throat virtually closing in on themselves and you have a good sense of how to make this sound. Remember these sets merge in *all* Standard English Accents, so be sure to make them rhyme!

THOUGHT: Paul applauded all the naughty daughters who yawned when taught with chalk and talk.

NORTH: George cavorted with Thor to fortify his short torso for the war in York.

FORCE: 'Of course I adore Nora', roared the porter through the door to the four divorced boarders.

FACE: Much like Traditional RP but with the added military tone and bark, this becomes a very tiny slide from the raised DRESS vowel to the raised KIT vowel, making it almost Extreme Vowel 2 (as in the French vowel in *du thé*). Thinking of it as a FLEECE vowel can help the tongue into position.

April felt faint as she campaigned to rein in the wasteful ladies to change their ways and obey.

GOAT–*GOAL*: This loses a lot of its slide. It sounds almost like a NURSE vowel or even a slide from DRESS to neutral schwa! Be sure to keep the same shape when the vowel is followed by 'L'!

Joan coaxed her beau, Owen, to grow **bold**er, though she loathed over-**controlling soldiers.**

PRICE: This vowel is snappy. Start almost from BATH (but keeping the jaw tight!) and snap immediately to a short FLEECE.

Friday is the right night to arrive by bicycle in Cyprus to buy a fine eiderdown.

CHOICE: Slide swiftly from LOT to a slightly tight KIT vowel.

The boy employed a joist to hoist the moist oysters into the boiling oil.

MOUTH: Start at BATH and slide to a schwa. Lose any lip-rounding from the second half of this slide. Some speakers slide a little more towards KIT, making POUND sound like PINED!

The loud crowd from south of the county wanted to oust the clown out of town, but they were all mouth.

NEAR: Almost identical to SQUARE in some speakers. Start from a raised DRESS (not quite KIT) and slide to the 'UH' or even the wide STRUT vowel.

Maria was sincere in her weird career, but feared the fierce bearded cashier.

SQUARE: Start from a slightly half-hearted DRESS vowel and flatten into the 'UH' or STRUT vowel.

Where the pears are scarce, the bears share theirs fairly.

TOUR: This set is a mixed bag. It is likely to split with some words merging with NURSE and some with THOUGHT. Play with both and see what you get and make a strong decision in one direction or the other.

> Muriel assured the poor tourists that the insurance was sure to cover Europe.

NB. See the note on page 145 regarding the PAW–POUR–POOR split!

Environmental Issues

Vowel Clusters and Collisions:

Smoothing: Extreme

A general feature of all upper-class accents is the use of smoothing to a greater or lesser degree.

'Smoothing' refers to the 'smoothing out' of the vowel slides that happen when two or more vowels from the KIT list meet.

For example, in the word 'science', the PRICE vowel meets the schwa, making a slide through three shapes: 'A–I–UH'. To smooth this slide out, remove the middle shape completely, losing any feeling of 'Y' from the tongue, leaving you with 'SA–UNCE' or even 'SAHNCE'.

This also happens when words meet… Try saying the following, losing any feeling of 'W' or 'Y' between these words:

> GO OUT   DO IT   PLAY ON

This accent uses *extreme* smoothing.

Hear It: Track 108.

> *fire* ('fa-i-uh') smoothes to 'fah'
>
> *power* ('pa-oo-uh') smoothes to 'pah'
>
> *throwing* ('thruh-oo-ing') smoothes to 'thruhng'

Vowels followed by 'ER' and 'ING' are the most common to be subject to smoothing:

> player   lawyer   mower   higher   tower
>
> fleeing   drawing   doing   playing   bowing   lying   annoying

GOING: The very forward position of the tongue at the start of the GOAT vowel means that when it is said quickly, without any stress, there is not even a hint of a 'W' or lip-rounding in the middle of this word. 'Going home' = 'gung hum' or 'geng hem'.

Hear It: *Track 109.*

We were **going** to a party in **Lower** Loxeley, bowling along with considerable **power, trying** to get to it on time. 'Who are we **seeing** there?' I asked. 'Oh, some very **annoying** people', he answered. 'There'll be **Howard**, the incessant card **player**, and my Aunt the **lawyer, doing** her usual party piece. They'll be in the **drawing** room, gathered around the **fire, chewing** the fat, **playing** "who is the smartest", **allowing** no one else to get a word in. How **tire**some!'

Vowel Reductions: The little sounds with a big impact!

When a syllable has no weight, or stress in it, the vowel is 'reduced' to something shorter and less open than it would be otherwise. How many syllables are reduced and which vowel is used can make a huge difference to the quality of the accent.

Older upper-class accents had a strong tendency to *minimise* the number of stressed syllables in a word, often stressing only one syllable in multisyllabic words. This means that vowels are being reduced left, right and centre!

Here are some key words that are stressed differently as a result:

Hear It: *Track 110.*

necessary = NEsusry   circumstances = CIRcumstunsiz
momentarily = MOmuntruly
finance = fiNANCE   portrait = PORtrut

This feature extends to *all* 'ORY', 'ARY', 'ONY', etc. endings:

inventory = INvuntry   library = LIbry   alimony = ALimuny

happY: This is a KIT vowel in most older upper-class accents, though in this accent it may be more open and close to a DRESS vowel or even a commA vowel, especially as a final sound of a phrase!

Hear It: *Track 111.*

Bill**y** and Mar**y** were happ**y** to see the mov**ie**, 'When Harry Met Sall**y**'. Bill**y** had a coff**ee**, and Mar**y** had a pastr**y**.

FLEECE and GOOSE vowels shorten to KIT and FOOT final unstressed positions:

He loves m**e**.   We shall b**e**.   Sh**e** was, was sh**e**?   Would y**ou**   The igl**oo**

commA–lettER: The schwa is very open and barked when it is in a final position.

Hear It: Track 112.

gather   writer   anger   India   Diana   yoga

privATE word endings:

These little endings have changed over time. In contemporary accents they have a commA vowel, but in older varieties they all had the KIT vowel:

Hear It: Track 113.

toil**et** (bracelet, pamphlet, etc.) = TOI-l*it*
priv**ate** (climate, etc.) = PRI-*vit*
probl**em** (system, Blenheim, etc.) = PROB-*lim*
kind**ness** (countless, business, etc.) = KIND-*niss*

horsES word endings:

The following little endings also use a KIT vowel in *all* varieties of Standard English, so watch out if your accent uses a commA vowel!

hors**es** (foxes, daises, marries, etc.) = HOR-*siz*
wast**ed** (landed, excited, etc.) = WAS-*tid*
long**est** (biggest, forest, etc.) = LONG-*gist*
act**ive** (massive, etc.) = AC- *tiv*
pock**et** (biscuit, planet) = PO-*kit*
coll**ege** (sausage, baggage, package, etc.) = CO-*lidge*
surf**ace** (office) = SUR-*fiss*

Finally, for our North American friends with good intentions, we must mention and draw attention to the convention of...

TION endings: It is crucial that these have a tiny schwa, and not a nasalised KIT vowel in them. This tiny detail can be a real giveaway! For example:

Hear It: Track 114.

attention = *attenshun*, not *attenshin*
mission = *misshun*, not *misshin*
station = *stayshun*, not *stayshin*

MM&LG

DEBS, DANDIES AND BRIGHT YOUNG THINGS

The FRAME

This is a sound that oozes sex appeal, sensuality and self-indulgence. It is a sound that may be heard in British actors during the 'Hollywood' years of the 1950s, but its origins were in a generation before that. Caught between the horrors of the First World War and the looming disaster of the Second emerged a generation of 'live for today' hedonists, dedicated to decadence, fun and frivolity. They used their position of privilege to live a life of indulgence, parties and champagne, breaking free from the rigidity of their Victorian parents in terms of style, music, language and behaviour. Much to the distaste of a bewildered older generation, they embraced the riotous music of American Swing Jazz with its improvisation, fast erratic tempos, lack of strings and occasionally risqué lyrics. This was the era of new dance crazes, the Charleston, The Jitterbug and the Lindy Hop, to name but a few. They loved to use slang expressions, nursery nicknames, and the language of extravagance, 'I'm awfully sorry, Piggy', 'Boo looks simply divine', 'Ghastly party, Loops!', which persisted well into the Sloane Rangers and It Crowd of the 1980s and 1990s. There was a relishing of wealth, danger and excess. Gone was the sense of continuity and responsibility. Life was to be both a sensation and sensational.

People: Anthony Andrews, Diana Dors, Fenella Fielding, Nigel Havers, Jack Hawkins, Hattie Jaques, Glynis Johns, Nancy Mitford, David Niven, Nicholas Parsons, Leslie Phillips, George Sanders, Terry-Thomas, Michael York.

Television/Film/Radio Characters: Wren Chasen and Lieutenant Phillips in *The Navy Lark* (BBC Radio, *Heather Chasen and Leslie Phillips*). The majority of the young English characters in *Vile Bodies* and *Bright Young Things!* Mrs Banks in *Mary Poppins* (*Glynis Johns*), Miranda in *Mad About Men* (*Glynis Johns*), Cordelia in *Brideshead Revisited* (*Phoebe Nicholls*).

Characters and Plays: Amanda and Elyot (*Private Lives*), Dickie Winslow (*The Winslow Boy*), Charles Lomax and Sarah Undershaft (*Major Barbara*), Lord Goring & Mabel Chiltern (*An Ideal Husband*), Joan Scott-Fowler (*After the Dance*), Lady Maureen Gilpin & Commander Peter Gilpin (*Hands across the Sea*), Viv and Maurice (*Tom and Viv*), Tuppy Glossop, Stinker Pinker, Stiffy Byng, Madeline Basset (PG Woodhouse, *Jeeves and Wooster*), Sorrel Bliss (*Hay Fever*), Felicity Rumpers (*Habeus Corpus*).

Hear it: Track 115. 'Arthur the Rat'.

The GROOVE

The rhythm is full of the influence of swing music. Whether slow or fast the momentum drives towards the key word in the phrase, where the voice lands, indulges, then swings off to the next.

In the tune anything goes, from the small range of the sexy bluesy tunes to the dramatic expressive expansions of bebop scatting through extremes of range. Individual expression reigns! A particular feature of both this, and the Sloane Rangers varieties, is the lengthening of a vowel and pitch-gliding *during* it for drama or emphasis.

Embody It

Physical Actions: Rhythmic gymnastics with the ribbon, the carefree elegance of Isadora Duncan's free flow dancing, or for moments of real abandon, the uninhibited dance moves of the Cotton Club!

Laban Actions: Indirect Flicks and Slashes landing in a direct Press.

See it:

FLICK   SLASH   PRESS

Hear it: Track 115. Listen for these qualities.

Feel It: This only really makes sense when you actually do it, so have a go. Imagine you have a huge gymnastics ribbon and swing it, or fling your arms with gay abandon!

Refine It

Hear It: Track 115. Listen to the line, 'There was once a young rat named Arthur, who could never take the trouble to make up his mind' and sing the tune you hear.

Feel it: Now combine the physical actions with the tune.

The FOUNDATIONS

Gone is the elegant, passive exterior, and in its place is a feeling of physical freedom and a general lack of apparent propriety. The facial muscles have a sense of surprise, shock or excitement in them, as if you breathed in suddenly with open-mouthed delight! There is a sensual awareness of the lips and the tongue, and the sensation of resonance.

Setting

Jaw and Cheeks: The jaw is free and cheeks have a slight lift, as if just on the edge of a smile.

Lips: The lips are slightly pouted, like plumped up pillows, with the top lip lifted and pushed out a little as if ready to kiss.

Tongue: The tongue is forward in the mouth, ready for the next indulgent taste, and pushing the sound into the mask of the face.

Soft Palate: The soft palate is a little high, lifting with a sense of surprise and anticipation but bouncy and responsive, not stiff.

Zone

See It:

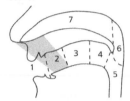

Aim the sound for Zone 2 and drive it through the gum-ridge into the philtrum, and also up into the eyes and cheekbones.

Tone

The resultant tone is like a jazz clarinet, full, rich and sexy.

Direction

See It:

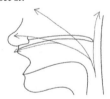

Drive the sound into your ears, eyes, nose and top lip. Think of all the senses being turned on by the sound.

Hesitation Sound

As a result of all the above, the relaxed sound of the mouth is a schwa that lifts slightly from the midpoint, towards the gum-ridge and buzzes into the roof of the mouth and onto the top lip.

See It: and *Hear It:* Watch the clips of Fenella Fielding and Glynis Johns at www.howtodoaccents.com

---

Putting it all together

Begin by counting to ten, focusing on maintaining the setting, zone, tone and direction.

Hear It: Track 116.

Increase this to days of the week, and months of the year, before trying a piece of text.

Planet Non-Rhotic

Remember, ALL Standard English Accents are Non-Rhotic! (see page 43).

You will hear linking 'Rs' (see page 45) in this variety:

> Fearand horror   search foranew home
> thereis room and good food forus all   underit they saw

...but probably not intrusive 'Rs' (see page 46):

> the idea of (not idea r of)   they saw a young rat (not saw r a)

Hear It: Track 117.

Listen to the above phrases from *Arthur the Rat* and hear those linking 'Rs' being put to good use, but not intrusive.

The BITE

Major Players

R L H NG TH

'R': Tap it lightly on the gum-ridge between vowels, especially between the front vowels such as KIT, DRESS and TRAP, both within words and between words:

> very   marry   here I go

NB. If you are using this variety for a more modern character, possibly from the 1950s, the 'R' may tap a lot less, and be replaced by a very weak 'R', with only the slightest gentle bend at the front of the tongue.

Major Issues

VOICING: Extra voicing means extra vibrations; extra vibrations means more sensation! As well as sitting in the 'Ms', 'Vs', 'Ns', 'Ls', 'Zs' and 'NGs', lingering in voiced sounds leads to the apparent adding of 'Ms', 'Ns' and 'NGs' before plosives in the weighty syllables. Sit in these nasal sounds before you continue:

Bobby = mBobby Debbie = nDebbie Gordon = ngGordon

Can NDeborah come?

nDo you come from nDeptford?

'T': Lift the tip of the tongue onto the gum-ridge, without any tension in the jaw at all, the teeth staying apart. It is a light delicate tap without any 'splash'.

Do take Dotty and Ted a better bit of butter for their tea and toast.

WHICH v WITCH: Unlike their parents, the bother of distinguishing 'WH' from 'W' is far too delicate, after all, why add air, when you can have full voice!

what–watt where–wear why–Y

which–witch whether–weather

'YOOs': On the other hand, here is an opportunity to *add* voice, so not only can you use these after *all* gum-ridge and dental consonants, but really indulge in the added length of these vowels!

Rather than be lewd, he presumed it was his duty to play a suitable tune with enthusiasm.

Try seeing the word either with a 'YOO' or with 'EE–OO' to help your mouth along.

lyood / lee-ood   prezyoomed / prezee-oomed

dyooty / dee-ooty   syootable / see-ootable

tyoon / tee-oon   enthyoosiasm / enthee-oosiasm

Hear It: Track 118. Listen to these Major Players and Major Issues and have a go yourself.

All the other Major Players and Issues are the same as a New Standard English Accent.

The SHAPES: —————————————————————————

A key feature of this variety (and also of the yet-to-be-born Sloane Rangers!) is the strong tendency to lengthen the traditionally *short* vowels of the KIT, DRESS, STRUT, FOOT, TRAP and LOT sets over a lovely pitch glide:

'It's hi–im!'   'He drives me round the be–end!'
'I lu–uve him!'   'Oh, did you read that boo–ok?'
'I feel so ba–ad about it!'   'I'm so frightfully ho–ot!'

Hear It: *Track 119.* 'The Kit List'.

KIT: This set has a shape that is closer to being a short version of a FLEECE vowel. Sprinkle a little 'EE' onto it, keep the sound bright, focus it onto the philtrum, high and forward, and spread the sound across the gum-ridge. Single syllable words can be stretched over a pitch glide for extra drama!

The ship listed as busy women built a pretty bridge in the dim mid-winter.

DRESS: The DRESS vowel has moved into the NSEA KIT territory, so imagine you are *almost* saying DRISS! Single syllable words can be stretched over a pitch glide for extra drama!

In a sweat (swit), Jeff (Jiff) edged (idged) his head (hid) into the Thames (Tims) in an effort (iffort) to save his best (bist) friend (frind) from the treacherous (tricherous) bell (bill) of death (dith).

STRUT: The open vertical setting gives a little extra space to this shape. Single syllable words can be stretched over a pitch glide for extra drama!

The dull young monks rushed in a flood to hunt the buds of the lovely buttercup.

FOOT: The hump in the tongue is high and quite far back which gives this a 'darker', lower quality than the New Standard English Accent. Be sure to round and pout the lips forward. To modern ears this will sound very close to a short GOOSE vowel. Single syllable words can be stretched over a pitch glide for extra drama!

The woman shouldn't put the full pudding onto the butcher's hook.

GOOSE: Maximise the full, deep 'owl-hoot' resonance with the back of the tongue high. Round and pout the lips, as if around a pencil. Use the *inner* muscle of the lip, and the thrust in the cheeks to push the lips forward while keeping them plump. Make a 'G' and then slightly release the tongue into the owl hoot to feel the back of the tongue in this raised position.

Two beautiful youths moved through a few smooth, juicy, rude grooves in feudal confusion.

FLEECE: This is almost as extreme as it can be. Keep it bright and sparkly by squeezing the hump in the tongue up the centre point of the gum-ridge.

The police had reason to believe that Peter, Keith and the anaemic Sheila could be in league to illegally deceive people.

NURSE: (No 'R'!) As with the hesitation sound, this vowel lifts slightly up from the midline towards the gum-ridge and buzzes onto the top lip. Sprinkle a little DRESS onto the sound. There is absolutely NO lip-rounding. If anything, the lips feel a *tiny* bit spread.

> Pearl urged Myrtle's attorney to rehearse a certain circus turn before the courteous worm turned.

TRAP: Imagine you are saying TREP, but be sure to open the jaw vertically, rather than using tight lips. Single syllable words can be stretched over a pitch glide for extra drama!

> The cat (ket) dashed (deshed) to catch (ketch) the ham (hem) that (thet) dangled (dengled) from the bag (beg).

BATH–PALM–START: (No 'R'!) Think of this shape as a little wider and further forward than Traditional RP; this gives it a lighter, brighter, less plummy quality. Remember these sets merge in *all* Standard English Accents, so be sure to make them rhyme!

> **BATH:** 'Francis the calf can't dance', laughed Sandra the giraffe, aghast, as the calf pranced disastrously.
>
> **PALM:** Brahms' sonata kept father calm in the spa.
>
> **START:** Sergeant Charles was the star of the party with his hearty aria.

LOT: Much like NSEA, the jaw is dropped open, while the cheeks are hollowed, and the lips rounded and pushing gently forward. There is a slight hump in the back of the tongue that shapes the sound. The resonance is at the back of the mouth and has a low quality. Single syllable words can be stretched over a pitch glide for extra drama. (NB. The words *was, because* and *of* are all in this set when they are stressed in a sentence!)

> Tom honestly acknowledged how top-notch the swan was to dodge the yacht.

CLOTH: After the Second World War this set began to merge with LOT, but in older accents/speakers it merged with THOUGHT, etc. The result was that during the 1940s, 1950s and 1960s some words hovered between the two sets! Single syllable words can be stretched over a pitch glide for extra drama!

Single syllable words where the vowel is followed by 'F' (*off*), 'S' (*cost*) and 'TH' (*cloth*) clung to the THOUGHT set the most stubbornly!

> Ross often frothed the coffee and washed the long sausages in Boston.

THOUGHT–NORTH–FORCE: (No 'R'!) Again this is much like the NSEA shape. From the LOT shape (described above), close the lips a little, like drawing the purse string very slightly tighter, engage the 'thrust muscle' of the cheeks a little more, and then add the *length* that really makes this vowel (yes, even in the THOUGHT sound, in spite of the lack of 'R'!). Remember these sets merge in *all* Standard English Accents, so be sure to make them rhyme!

THOUGHT: Paul applauded all the naughty daughters who yawned when taught with chalk and talk.

NORTH: George cavorted with Thor to fortify his short torso for the war in York.

FORCE: 'Of course I adore Nora', roared the porter through the door to the four divorced boarders.

NB. The *momentum* in the following sliding shapes is a key feature of this variety. Swing in to the first shape and out on the second. The volume, energy and muscularity all gather in the first half and fade in the second. While you are swinging and sliding in the shape you can also slide over the notes too!

FACE: This becomes a very tiny slide from the raised DRESS vowel to the raised KIT vowel. You could almost think of it as a FLEECE vowel to help the tongue into position.

April felt faint as she campaigned to rein in the wasteful ladies to change their ways and obey.

GOAT–GOAL: Start from the slightly forward schwa, with a little preparatory lip-rounding, and slide to the FOOT vowel. And be sure to use exactly the same sound and shape in the GOAL words, too (shown in **bold**):

Joan coaxed her beau, Owen, to grow **bold**er, though she loathed over-**controlling soldiers.**

PRICE: Push this slide a little further forward in the mouth than in a NSEA to keep it bright and sparkly! Swing in on a relaxed TRAP shape and out on a KIT. Remember, this is your personal pronoun, 'I', so be sure to anchor this sound to your centre and connect it to your sense of self.

Friday is the right night to arrive by bicycle in Cyprus to buy a fine eiderdown.

CHOICE: Unlike the NSEA, this starts from the LOT shape (as described above), not a THOUGHT shape, and only slides to KIT. Again, swing in on the LOT and off on the KIT.

The boy employed a joist to hoist the moist oysters into the boiling oil.

MOUTH: Swing in on the BATH shape and off half-heartedly on FOOT.

The loud crowd from south of the county wanted to oust the clown out of town, but they were all mouth.

NEAR: Swing in from a KIT shape and off on a schwa.

Maria was sincere in her weird career, but feared the fierce bearded cashier.

SQUARE: Swing in on a slightly raised DRESS and slide to the schwa.

Where the pears are scarce, the bears share theirs fairly.

TOUR: (NO 'R'!) In older accents this was a set that didn't merge with NURSE or THOUGHT, but was a set of its own. Words in this set had a lovely little slide from the foot vowel to the schwa. Like blowing a kiss.

Muriel assured the poor tourists that the insurance was sure to cover Europe.

NB. See the note on page 145 regarding the PAW–POUR–POOR split!

Environmental Issues:

Vowel Clusters and Collisions:

Smoothing: Extreme!

A general feature of all upper-class accents is the use of smoothing to a greater or lesser degree.

'Smoothing' refers to the 'smoothing out' of the vowel slides that happen when two or more vowels from the Kit List meet.

For example, in the word 'science', the PRICE vowel meets the schwa, making a slide through three shapes: 'A–I–UH'. To smooth this slide out, remove the middle shape completely, losing any feeling of 'Y' from the tongue, leaving you with 'SA–UNCE' or even 'SAHNCE'.

This also happens when words meet… Try saying the following, losing any feeling of 'W' or 'Y' between these words:

GO OUT   DO IT   PLAY ON

This variety uses *extreme* smoothing.

Hear It: Track 120.

fire ('fa-i-uh') smoothes to 'fah'

power ('pa-oo-uh') smoothes to 'pah'

throwing ('thruh-oo-ing') smoothes to 'thruhng'

Vowels followed by 'ER' and 'ING' are the most common to be subject to smoothing:

player   lawyer   mower   higher   tower

fleeing   drawing   doing   playing   bowing   lying   annoying

GOING. The very forward position of the tongue at the start of the GOAT vowel means that when it is said quickly, without any stress, there is not even a hint of a 'W' or lip-rounding in the middle of this word. 'Going home' = 'gung hum' or 'geng hem'.

Hear It: *Track 121.*

> We were **going** to a party in **Lower** Loxeley, bowling along with considerable **power, trying** to get to it on time. 'Who are we **seeing** there?' I asked. 'Oh, some very **annoying** people', he answered. 'There'll be **Howard**, the incessant card **player**, and my Aunt the **lawyer, doing** her usual party piece. They'll be in the **drawing** room, gathered around the **fire, chewing** the fat, **playing** "who is the smartest", **allowing** no one else to get a word in. How **tire**some!'

Vowel Reductions: The little sounds with a big impact!

When a syllable has no weight or stress in it, the vowel is 'reduced' to something shorter and less open than it would be otherwise. How many syllables are reduced, and which vowel is used can make a huge difference to the quality of the accent.

Older upper-class accents had a strong tendency to *minimise* the number of stressed syllables in a word, often stressing only one syllable in multisyllabic words. This means that vowels are being reduced left, right and centre!

Here are some key words that are stressed differently as a result:

Hear It: *Track 122.*

> necessary = NEsusry   circumstances = CIRcumstunsiz
> momentarily = MOmuntruly   finance = fiNANCE
> portrait = PORtrut

This feature extends to *all* 'ORY', 'ARY', 'ONY', etc. endings:

> inventory = INvuntry   library = LIbry   alimony = ALimuny

happY: This little ending is a KIT vowel in older upper-class accents:

Hear It: *Track 123.*

> Billy and Mary were happy to see the movie, 'When Harry Met Sally'.
> Billy had a coffee, and Mary bought a pastry.

FLEECE and **GOOSE** vowels shorten to KIT and FOOT final unstressed positions:

> He loves me   We shall be   She was, was she?   Would you   The igloo

commA–lettER: Use a slightly raised schwa:

Hear It: Track 124.

gather   writer   anger   India   Diana   yoga

privATE word endings: These little endings have changed over time. In contemporary accents they have a commA vowel, but in older varieties they all had the KIT vowel:

Hear It: Track 125.

toil**et** (bracelet, pamphlet, etc.) = TOI-l*it*
priv**ate** (climate, etc.) = PRI-*vit*
probl**em** (system, Blenheim, etc.) = PROB-*lim*
kind**ness** (countless, business, etc.) = KIND-*niss*

horsES word endings: The following little endings also use a KIT vowel in *all* varieties of Standard English, so watch out if your accent uses a commA vowel!

hors**es** (foxes, daises, marries, etc.) = HOR-*siz*
wast**ed** (landed, excited, etc.) = WAS-*tid*
long**est** (biggest, forest, etc.) = LONG-*gist*
act**ive** (massive, etc.) = AC- *tiv*
pock**et** (biscuit, planet) = PO-*kit*
coll**ege** (sausage, baggage, package, etc.) = CO-*lidge*
sur**face** (office) = SUR-*fiss*

Finally, for our North American friends with good intentions, we must mention and draw attention to the convention of...

TION endings: It is crucial that these have a tiny commA vowel, and not a nasalised KIT vowel in them. This tiny detail can be a real giveaway! For example:

Hear It: Track 126.

attention = *attenshun*, not *attenshin*
mission = *misshun*, not *misshin*
station = *stayshun*, not *stayshin*

WARTIME WENDIES AND BBC BERTIES

The FRAME

The socially equalizing effects of the Second World War gave rise to an expanding middle class dedicated to self-improvement. They were also the first generation of people to have grown up listening to the BBC. Postwar Britain was a place where humility, hard work, austerity and self-control were valued. Personal emotional indulgence was not. Gone are the days of luxuriating in the trappings of wealth; this is the time of the expansion of suburbia and the civil service. Think ration books, stiff upper lips, and a 'make do and mend' mentality.

People: Celia Johnson, John Snagge, John Mills, Sylvia Peters, Trevor Howard, Jack Hawkins, Sheila Sim, Cyril Raymond, Clement Attlee, Annette Mills, Googie Withers, Joyce Grenfell, Dulcie Gray, Gwen Watford, Lionel Gamlin, Leslie Mitchell, Bob Danvers-Walker (*Pathé Pictorial announcers*), Raymond Glendenning (*BBC commentator and sports announcer*).

Television/Film Radio Characters: Laura Jesson, Fred Jesson, Dr Alec Harvey (*Brief Encounter*), Mrs Kinross (*In Which We Serve*), RAF Pilots (*Armstrong and Miller* comedy sketch show), Lavinia Dakers and Rachel Hammond (*My Brother Jonathan 1948*), and many characters in *The Cruel Sea*, *The Dambusters*, *The 39 Steps*.

Characters and Plays: Laura Jesson, Fred Jesson, Dr Alec Harvey (*Still Life*), Richard Hannay and Pamela (*The 39 Steps*), Charles Condomine and Ruth (*Blithe Spirit*), Mollie Ralston (*The Mousetrap*), Midge Hardcastle (*The Hollow*), Patricia (*Flare Path*).

Hear it: Track *127*. 'Arthur the Rat'.

The GROOVE

The indulgent pace and rhythm of the Imperial Lords and Ladies and the Bright Young Things is a thing of the past. It is replaced with a very rapid pace and staccato rhythms.

The tune is almost like a newsreader, following very standard patterns, avoiding emotional outburst at all costs, stepping up and down within a fairly narrow range with occasional swoops as the emotion escapes.

Embody It

Physical Actions: Secretarial typing on an old typewriter, or military drumming, may all help evoke the feeling of the Groove in the body.

Laban Actions: Dab.

See it:

DAB

Hear it: Track 127. Listen for these qualities.

Feel It: This only really makes sense when you actually do it, so have a go. Imagine you are typing, or drumming to get the Groove into your body.

Refine It

Hear It: Track 127. Listen to the line 'There was once a young rat named Arthur, who could never take the trouble to make up his mind' and sing the tune you hear.

Feel it: Now combine the physical actions with the tune.

The FOUNDATIONS

There is a bound, held feeling in the body and the face, with a sense of seriousness or even severity in the facial muscles. The cheeks feel a little raised, as if holding a half-smile through all the hardship and severity.

Setting

Jaw and Cheeks: The jaw bounces lightly within a small range to allow the speed of utterance. The feeling of looseness in the cheeks has gone and is replaced with a slight lift, as if on the edge of a smile.

Lips: The top lip is held up in a slight, stiff pucker from which the lips work in a small band, back and forth. Imagine looking from the side and seeing the lips pushing forward and back, but keep the movement to its absolute minimum!

Tongue: The tongue tip is extremely precise and accurate, almost magnetically drawn to a point in the centre of the gum-ridge. The tongue sits forward in the mouth in a state of alert. Suck air into your mouth as if through a straw to get the feeling in the tongue.

Soft Palate: Bouncy, alert and active. Though the space in the mouth is a little small, the active, alert soft palate ensures that the sound does not become dull or overly nasalised.

Zone: 1-2

See It:

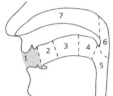

Tone

The resultant tone is like a broody chicken playing an oboe!

Direction

See It:

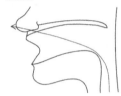

Straight through the gum-ridge and into the nostrils.

Hesitation Sound

Slightly forward, tight schwa...sprinkle some DRESS on it.

Putting it all together

Begin by counting to ten, focusing on maintaining the setting, zone, tone and direction.

Hear It: Track 128. Hesitation sound followed by numbers.

Increase this to days of the week, and months of the year, before trying a piece of text.

Planet Non-Rhotic ─────────────

Remember, ALL Standard English Accents are Non-Rhotic! (see page 43). You will hear linking 'Rs' (see page 45) in this variety:

Hear It: Track 129.

search fora new home

thereis room and good food forus all   underit they saw

...but probably not intrusive 'Rs' (see page 46)...

they saw a young rat (not saw r a)   the idea of (not idea r of)

WW&BBC

The BITE

Major Players

R L H NG TH

'**R**': Taps lightly on the gum-ridge between vowels, especially between the front vowels such as KIT, DRESS and TRAP, both within words and between words:

very   marry   here I go

Major Issues

T: Lift the tip of the tongue onto the gum-ridge, without any tension in the jaw at all, the teeth staying apart. It is a light, delicate tap.

Do take Dotty and Ted a better bit of butter for their tea and toast.

WHICH v WITCH: Distinguish words with 'WH' by adding a slight puff of air through the lips before the 'W', almost like 'hwat', 'hwere', etc. NB. Careful, don't overdo this, it is very gentle in this accent:

what–watt   where–wear   why–Y
which–witch   whether–weather

'**YOOs**': After *all* gum-ridge and dental consonants.

Rather than be lewd, he presumed it was his duty to play a suitable tune with enthusiasm.

Try seeing the word either with a 'YOO' or with 'EE–OO' to help your mouth along.

lyood / lee-ood   prezyoomed / prezee-oomed
dyooty / dee-ooty   syootable / see-ootable
tyoon / tee-oon   enthyoosiasm / enthee-oosiasm

Hear It: *Track 130.* Listen to these Major Players and the Major Issues and have a go yourself.

All the other Major Players and Major Issues are the same as NSEA.

The SHAPES

The Foundations give many of the shapes a crisp, bright quality.

Hear It: *Track 131.* 'The Kit List'.

KIT: This set has a shape that is closer to being a short version of a FLEECE vowel. Sprinkle a little 'EE' onto it, keep the sound snappy and bright, and focus it tightly onto the centre point of the gum-ridge.

The ship listed as busy women built a pretty bridge in the dim mid-winter.

DRESS: The DRESS vowel has moved into the NSEA KIT territory, so imagine you are *almost* saying DRISS!

In a sweat (swit), Jeff (Jiff) edged (idged) his head (hid) into the Thames (Tims) in an effort (iffort) to save his best (bist) friend (frind) from the treacherous (tricherous) bell (bill) of death (dith).

STRUT: Sprinkle a little TRAP onto this shape, keeping it bright and snappy.

The dull young monks rushed in a flood to hunt the buds of the lovely buttercup.

FOOT: The hump in the tongue is high and quite far back which gives this a 'darker', lower quality than the NSEA. Be sure to round and pout the lips forward. To modern ears this will sound very close to a short GOOSE vowel.

The woman shouldn't put the full pudding onto the butcher's hook.

GOOSE: Maximise the full, deep 'owl-hoot' resonance with the back of the tongue high (make a 'G' and then slightly release the tongue to feel the back of the tongue in its raised position). Round and pout the lips. Use the inner muscle of the lip to push the lips forward a little.

Two beautiful youths moved through a few smooth, juicy, rude grooves in feudal confusion.

FLEECE: This is almost as extreme as it can be. Keep it bright and sparkly by squeezing the hump in the tongue up the centre point of the gum-ridge, and fill up the resonance behind it.

The police had reason to believe that Peter, Keith and the anaemic Sheila could be in league to illegally deceive people.

NURSE: (No 'R'!) As with the hesitation sound, this vowel lifts slightly up from the midline, towards the gum-ridge and buzzes onto the top lip. Sprinkle a little DRESS onto the sound. There is absolutely NO lip-rounding. If anything, the lips feel a *tiny* bit spread.

Pearl urged Myrtle's attorney to rehearse a certain circus turn before the courteous worm turned.

TRAP: Imagine you are saying TREP, but be sure to open the jaw vertically, rather than using tight lips. This is one of the most noticeable changes in this accent.

> The cat (ket) dashed (deshed) to catch (ketch) the ham (hem) that (thet) dangled (dengled) from the bag (beg).

BATH–PALM–START: (No 'R'!) Think of this shape as a little wider and further forward than Traditional RP; this gives it a lighter, brighter, less plummy quality. Remember these sets merge in *all* Standard English accents, so be sure to make them rhyme!

> **BATH:** 'Francis the calf can't dance', laughed Sandra the giraffe, aghast, as the calf pranced disastrously.
>
> **PALM:** Brahms' sonata kept father calm in the spa.
>
> **START:** Sergeant Charles was the star of the party with his hearty aria.

LOT: Hollow the cheeks and push the lips gently forward, but don't over-open the jaw in this variety. Try to create the space on the inside while maintaining that external control! Keep it snappy, this is a short vowel. In some actors of the period the shape heads a little closer to an American sound, with more relaxed lip-rounding, perhaps as a result of the influence of American movies. (NB. The words *was*, *because* and *of* are all in this set when they are stressed in a sentence!)

> Tom honestly acknowledged how top-notch the swan was to dodge the yacht.

CLOTH: After the Second World War, this set began to merge with LOT, but in older accents/speakers it merged with THOUGHT, etc. The result was that during the 1940s, 1950s and 1960s some words hovered between the two sets!

Single syllable words where the vowel is followed by 'F' (*off*), 'S'(*cost*) and 'TH' (*cloth*) clung to the THOUGHT set the most stubbornly!

> Ross often frothed the coffee and washed the long sausages in Boston.

THOUGHT–NORTH–FORCE: Be sure to make these all rhyme. Get the length in the THOUGHT sound, in spite of the lack of 'R'. Engage the 'thrust muscle' of the cheeks a little.

> **THOUGHT:** Paul applauded all the naughty daughters who yawned when taught them of war with chalk and talk.
>
> **NORTH:** George cavorted with Thor to fortify his short torso for the war in York.
>
> **FORCE:** 'Of course I adore Nora', roared the porter through the door to the four divorced boarders.

FACE: This becomes a very tiny slide from the raised DRESS vowel to the raised KIT vowel. You could almost think of it as a FLEECE vowel to help the tongue into position.

April felt faint as she campaigned to rein in the wasteful ladies to change their ways and obey.

GOAT–*GOAL*: For 'native' speakers start from the slightly forward schwa, with a little preparatory lip-rounding, and slide to the FOOT vowel. For a trained BBC reporter sound you may prefer to use the old Stage Standard shape. Start from the LOT shape and slide to FOOT. Whichever you do, be sure to use exactly the same sound and shape in the GOAL words, too (shown in **bold**):

Joan coaxed her beau, Owen, to grow **bolde**r, though she loathed over-**controlling soldiers.**

PRICE: Push this slide a little further forward in the mouth than NSEA to keep it bright and sparkly! Remember, this is your personal pronoun, 'I', so be sure to anchor this sound to your centre and connect it to your sense of self.

Friday is the right night to arrive by bicycle in Cyprus to buy a fine eiderdown.

CHOICE: Unlike the NSEA, this starts from the LOT shape (as described above), not a THOUGHT shape, and only slides to KIT. Again, put a little more weight in the first half of the slide:

The boy employed a joist to hoist the moist oysters into the boiling oil.

MOUTH: Start from BATH and slide to FOOT. This gives slide a much richer, lower resonant quality than is heard in more modern accents:

The loud crowd from south of the county wanted to oust the clown out of town, but they were all mouth.

NEAR: Start from the raised KIT and slide to the schwa:

Maria was sincere in her weird career, but feared the fierce bearded cashier.

SQUARE: Start from the raised DRESS and slide to the schwa:

Where the pears are scarce, the bears share theirs fairly.

TOUR: In *all* the older accents this was a set of its own. Words in this set had a lovely little slide from the FOOT vowel to the schwa.

Muriel assured the poor tourists that the insurance was sure to cover Europe.

NB. See the note on page 145 regarding the PAW–POUR–POOR split.

Environmental Issues: ————————————————

Vowel Clusters and Collisions:

Smoothing: Gentle.

A general feature of all upper-class accents is the use of smoothing to a greater or lesser degree.

'Smoothing' refers to the 'smoothing out' of the vowel slides that happen when two or more vowels from the Kit List meet.

For example, in the word 'science', the PRICE vowel meets the schwa, making a slide through three shapes: 'A–I–UH'. To smooth this slide out, remove the middle shape completely, losing any feeling of 'Y' from the tongue, leaving you with 'SA–UNCE' or even 'SAHNCE'.

This also happens when words meet… Try saying the following, losing any feeling of 'W' or 'Y' between these words:

GO OUT   DO IT   PLAY ON

This variety uses only *gentle* smoothing.

Hear It: Track 132.

fire ('fa-i-uh') smoothes to 'fa-uh'

power ('pa-oo-uh') smoothes to 'pa-uh'

throwing ('thruh-oo-ing') smoothes to 'thruh-ing'

Vowels followed by 'ER' and 'ING' are the most common to be subject to smoothing:

player   lawyer   mower   higher   tower   fleeing
drawing   doing   playing   bowing   lying   annoying

GOING: The very forward position of the tongue at the start of the GOAT vowel means that when it is said quickly, without any stress, there is not even a hint of a 'W' or lip-rounding in the middle of this word. 'Going home' = 'gung hum' or 'geng hem'.

Hear It: Track 133.

We were **going** to a party in **Lower** Loxeley, bowling along with considerable **power, trying** to get to it on time. 'Who are we **seeing** there?' I asked. 'Oh, some very **annoying** people', he answered. 'There'll be **Howard**, the incessant card **player**, and my Aunt the **lawyer, doing** her usual party piece. They'll be in the **drawing** room, gathered around the **fire, chewing** the fat, **playing** "who is the smartest", **allowing** no one else to get a word in. How **tire**some!'

Vowel Reductions: The little sounds with a big impact!

When a syllable has no weight, or stress in it, the vowel is 'reduced' to something shorter and less open than it would be otherwise. How many syllables are reduced and which vowel is used can make a huge difference to the quality of the accent.

Older upper-class accents had a strong tendency to *minimise* the number of stressed syllables in a word, often stressing only one syllable in multisyllabic words. That means that vowels are being reduced left, right and centre! (Track 89). But as the accent was adopted by more of the middle classes, some of these syllables returned.

Here are some key words that are stressed differently as a result:

Hear It: Track 134.

    necessary = NEsuSERy   circumstances = CIRcumSTAHNsiz
    momentarily = MOmuntruly   finance = fiNANCE
    portrait = PORtrut

This feature extends to *all* 'ORY', 'ARY', 'ONY', etc. endings:

    inventory = INvuntry   library = LIbry   alimony = ALimuny

happY: This is a very short KIT vowel in this variety.

Hear It: Track 135.

    Billy and Mary were happy to see the movie, 'When Harry Met Sally'. Billy
    had a coffee, and Mary bought a pastry.

FLEECE and **GOOSE** vowels shorten to KIT and FOOT final unstressed positions:

    He loves me   We shall be   She was, was she?   Would you   The igloo

commA–lettER: Use a slightly raised schwa, sprinkle some DRESS on it and keep it short and bright.

Hear It: Track 136.

    gather   writer   anger   India   Diana   yoga

privATE word endings: These little endings have changed over time. In contemporary accents they have a commA vowel, but in older varieties they all had the KIT vowel:

Hear It: Track 137.

    toil**et** (bracelet, pamphlet, etc.) = TOI-l*it*
    priv**ate** (climate, etc.) = PRI-*vit*

WW&BBC

problem (system, Blenheim, etc.) = PROB-*lim*

kind**ness** (countless, business, etc.) = KIND-*niss*

horsES word endings: The following little endings also use a KIT vowel in *all* varieties of Standard English, so watch out if your accent uses a commA vowel!

hors**es** (foxes, daises, marries, etc.) = HOR-*siz*

wast**ed** (landed, excited, etc.) = WAS-*tid*

long**est** (biggest, forest, etc.) = LONG-*gist*

act**ive** (massive, etc.) = AC-*tiv*

pock**et** (biscuit, planet) = PO-*kit*

coll**ege** (sausage, baggage, package, etc.) = CO-*lidge*

surf**ace** (office) = SUR-*fiss*

Finally, for our North American friends with good intentions, we must mention and draw attention to the convention of…

TION endings: It is crucial that these have a tiny commA vowel, and not a nasalised KIT vowel in them. This tiny detail can be a real giveaway! For example:

Hear It: Track 138.

attention = *attenshun*, not *attenshin*

mission = *misshun*, not *misshin*

station = *stayshun*, not *stayshin*

THE ORIGINAL SLOANE RANGERS

The FRAME

During the 1960s and 1970s there was a cultural celebration of the working classes in Britain. Popular television series such as *On The Buses, Love Thy Neighbour* and many of the *Carry On* films encapsulate this. But by the 1980s, with the rise of Thatcher and the young Tories, wealth and status were back in fashion. It was 'OK Ya!' to be posh (*Dynasty, Howard's Way*). In 1982 British writer Peter York and co-writer Ann Barr coined the term 'Sloane Ranger'. It combines the name of the character The Lone Ranger with the Chelsea location of Sloane Square, and was used as a label for the young and fashionably wealthy who frequented that area. Unlike their parents, many of this generation (though by no means all), had to work to earn money, giving rise to a work hard, play hard culture that embraced fast cars, champagne, big hair, and even bigger shoulder pads. But holding it all together was an essentially cool, laid-back facade.

People: Diana Princess of Wales, Earl Spencer, Liz Hurley, Kristin Scott Thomas, Helena Bonham Carter, Richard E. Grant.

TV/Film Characters: Charles, Duck Face and Fiona (Hugh Grant, Anna Chancellor and Kristin Scott Thomas in *Four Weddings and a Funeral*), Tim 'Nice But Dim' (*Harry Enfield*), Vanessa Kensington (Liz Hurley, *Austin Powers*), Withnail (Richard E. Grant, *Withnail and I*), Patsy Stone and Edina Monsoon (*Absolutely Fabulous*), Hugh Laurie (*Blackadder*).

Plays and Characters: Jake and Scilla (*Serious Money*, Caryl Churchill), Marlene (*Top Girls*, Caryl Churchill), all ten members of the Riot Club in *Posh* (Laura Wade), Princess Diana (*The Queen and I*, Sue Townsend), Kirsten and Phillip (*Gasping*, Ben Elton).

Hear it: Track 139. 'Arthur the Rat'.

SLOANE

The GROOVE

Some of the Grooves that arose during this period have much in common with East Coast American sounds (though the notorious up-speak of the 2000s has not yet taken hold!). The rhythm is surprisingly slow and evenly weighted through the phrase, lacking the strong distinctions between the heavy Landing Points and all the fast little unimportant syllables that typify earlier varieties of upper middle-class speech.

The tune has moved away from the large range and major cadences of the past into a very narrow range using small minor cadences. This can have the effect of making someone sound somewhat cool, disinterested, or even bored.

Embody It

Physical Actions: Think of smoke rising from a cigarette, or imagine punting (a favourite Sloane Ranger pastime), pushing the weight into the pole, feeding it through to the end of the line, but somehow still having a wonderful feeling of gently drifting along.

Laban Actions: Float and Glide.

 See It:

FLOAT   GLIDE

 Hear it: Track 139. Listen for these qualities.

Feel It: This only really makes sense when you actually do it, so have a go. Imagine you are smoke drifting around the room, or that you are punting to get the Groove into your body.

Refine It

 Hear It: Track 139. Listen to the line, 'There was once a young rat named Arthur, who could never take the trouble to make up his mind' and sing the tune you hear.

 Feel It: Now combine the words with the physical actions and the tune.

The FOUNDATIONS ─────────────────

The overall feeling in the body and face is one of elegance and languor with bright flirtatious eyes. There is a looseness, an indirectness, a floppy 'morning after the night before' quality in the muscles and movements.

Setting

Jaw and Cheeks: The jaw and cheeks are loose and floppy. Drop your jaw and release your chin, letting it fall back towards your neck.

Lips: These are pretty inactive, truth be told. Let them just lie there!

Tongue: The tongue is much flatter and a little heavier than in other varieties. There is much less definition in the movement from the front vowels to the back, leading to a centralising effect on many of them.

Soft Palate: Raise as if on the edge of a yawn. Imagine you have just eaten some hot potato. You are too polite to spit it out, so raise the soft palate and talk around it!

Zone: 3-5

See It:

Tone

The resultant tone is smoky, a little like a flute playing the low notes.

Direction

See It:

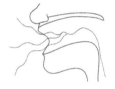

Drifts forward out of the mouth like smoke or steam, with the occasional active puff.

Hesitation Sound

As a result of the above the relaxed mouth produces an 'AH'-like vowel.

Putting it all together

Begin by counting to ten, focusing on maintaining the setting, zone, tone and direction.

Hear It: Track 140. Hesitation sound followed by numbers.

Increase this to days of the week, and months of the year, before trying a piece of text.

The Planet Non-Rhotic ───────────────

Remember, ALL Standard English Accents are Non-Rhotic! (see page 43). You will hear linking 'Rs' (see page 45) in this variety:

> Fearand horror   search fora new home
> thereis room and good food forus all   underit they saw

…and a *very* gentle intrusive 'R' (see page 46) after a schwa:

> the idea r of

SLOANE

...and possibly not after 'AW', though it is possible, but again with only the gentlest of bends in the tongue, and by no means any bounce in it.

they saw a young rat (not saw r a)

Hear It: *Track 141.*

Listen to the above phrases from *Arthur the Rat* and hear those linking 'Rs' being put to good use, but only the very gentlest of intrusives.

The BITE

Major Players

R L H NG TH

'R': The tapping of the 'R' has been consigned to history. In this variety the 'R' has a tendency to be extremely light. Use only the barest bend at the front of the tongue. In fact it often slips completely and becomes a weak 'R', made only by bringing the bottom lip up towards the top teeth, as if about to say a 'V'!

very   marry   here I go

Major Issues

'T': The tongue has to lift through the floppy open space to find the gum-ridge. The contact is softer than in Traditional RP, and between vowels it can even be a 'D', following on from the notion of American 'cool' speak.

Do take Dotty and Ted a bett(d)er bit(d) of butt(d)er for their tea and toast.

WHICH v WITCH: Gone are the days of the 'WH', these pairs are now identical.

what–watt   where–wear   why–Y
which–witch   whether–weather

'YOOs': You *can* use these after all gum-ridge and dental consonants, though by now it is much less likely to be used after 'S' (suit = *soot*) and may even crunch after 'T' (tune = *choon*) and 'D' (duty = *jewty*).

Rather than be lewd, he presumed it was his duty to play a (suit)able tune with enthusiasm.

Try seeing the word either with a 'YOO' or with 'EE–OO' to help your mouth along.

lyood / lee-ood   prezyoomed / prezee-oomed

dyooty / dee-ooty   (syootable /see-ootable)

tyoon / tee-oon   enthyoosiasm / enthee-oosiasm

Hear It: Track 142. Listen to these Major Players and Major Issues and have a go yourself.

All the other Major Players and Major Issues are the same as a NSEA.

The SHAPES

A key feature of this variety (and also of the Debs and Dandies) is the strong tendency to lengthen the traditionally *short* vowels of the KIT, DRESS, STRUT, FOOT, TRAP and LOT sets over a lovely pitch glide:

'It's hi-im!'   'He drives me round the be-end!'   'I lu-uve him!'

'Oh, did you read that boo-ok?'   'I feel so ba-ad about it!'

'I'm so frightfully ho-ot!'

Hear It: Track 143. 'The Kit List'.

KIT: Let this drop and flatten towards DRESS and the schwa, lurking somewhere in the territory between all three!

The ship listed as busy women built a pretty bridge in the dim mid-winter.

DRESS: Flatten the tongue from the Traditional RP shape. Sprinkle a little TRAP onto it.

In a sweat, Jeff edged his head into the Thames in an effort to save his best friend from the treacherous bell of death.

STRUT: Definitely think 'AH', just a little shorter.

The dull young monks rushed in a flood to hunt the buds of the lovely buttercup.

FOOT: More like the Military sound, this is not as completely far back as Traditional RP, it is much more similar to NSEA, moving towards the middle of the mouth, with reluctant, somewhat flattened lip-rounding.

The woman shouldn't put the full pudding onto the butcher's hook.

GOOSE: As with FOOT, this lacks some of the beautiful owl resonance of Traditional RP, though when compared with the New Wave (page 201) it is still considerably far back. Again the lips have reluctant, flattened rounding.

Two beautiful youths moved through a few smooth, juicy, rude grooves in feudal confusion.

SLOANE

FLEECE: Very tight, and often quite sudden in nature, shoot the sound onto the gum-ridge!

The police had reason to believe that Peter, Keith and the anaemic Sheila could be in league to illegally deceive people.

NURSE: (No 'R') As with the hesitation sound, this is really close to a BATH shape.

Pearl urged Myrtle's attorney to rehearse a certain circus turn before the courteous worm turned.

TRAP: In many speakers this has less of the 'TREP' quality associated with Traditional RP and is more similar to NSEA.

The cat dashed to catch the ham that dangled from the bag.

BATH–PALM–START: (No 'R'!) This isn't that different in shape from Traditional RP and a NSEA. It's an open vowel, with relaxed cheeks and lips, and an 'AH' quality. Keep the jaw open and relaxed, the vowel towards the back of the tongue, but not too plummy! Remember these sets merge in *all* Standard English Accents, so be sure to make them rhyme!

BATH: 'Francis the calf can't dance', laughed Sandra the giraffe, aghast, as the calf pranced disastrously.

PALM: Brahms' sonata kept father calm in the spa.

START: Sergeant Charles was the star of the party with his hearty aria.

LOT–CLOTH: This set has fully merged in this variety. Sadly the days of the *clawths*, *awfs* and *lawsts* are over. Don't overuse the lips. Make the tongue do the work, with the back raising and tensing slightly from the BATH shape.

LOT: Tom honestly acknowledged how top-notch the swan was to dodge the yacht.

CLOTH: Ross often frothed the coffee and washed the long sausages in Boston.

THOUGHT–NORTH–FORCE: (No 'R'!) Again this is much like the NSEA shape. From the LOT shape (described above), close the lips a little, like drawing the purse string very slightly tighter, engage the 'thrust muscle' of the cheeks a little more, and then add the *length* that really makes this vowel (yes, even in the THOUGHT sound, in spite of the lack of 'R'!). Remember these sets merge in *all* Standard English Accents, so be sure to make them rhyme!

THOUGHT: Paul applauded all the naughty daughters who yawned when taught with chalk and talk.

NORTH: George cavorted with Thor to fortify his short torso for the war in York.

FORCE: 'Of course I adore Nora', roared the porter through the door to the four divorced boarders.

FACE: Start from the open, flattened DRESS shape, and loosely slide towards the flattened KIT. It may almost feel like a long DRESS shape!

April felt faint as she campaigned to rein in the wasteful ladies to change their ways and obey.

GOAT–GOAL: Think of this as a long, flattened DRESS shape or a slightly forward schwa.

Joan coaxed her beau, Owen, to grow **bolder**, though she loathed over-**controlling soldiers.**

PRICE: Start from the BATH shape and slide smoothly and swiftly to the flattened KIT. Remember, this is your personal pronoun, 'I', so be sure to anchor this sound to your centre and connect it to your sense of self.

Friday is the right night to arrive by bicycle in Cyprus to buy a fine eiderdown.

CHOICE: Start from the loose LOT shape (described above), with a little more weight in the first shape, and slide smoothly to the flattened KIT.

The boy employed a joist to hoist the moist oysters into the boiling oil.

MOUTH: Start from BATH and slide without lip-rounding, to the schwa. (Like the Military variety, this can sometimes slide towards KIT making POUND sound like PINED.)

The loud crowd from south of the county wanted to oust the clown out of town, but they were all mouth.

NEAR: Start from a flattened KIT and slide smoothly home to a loose open schwa, with a good dose of 'AH' sprinkled on it!

Maria was sincere in her weird career, but feared the fierce bearded cashier.

SQUARE: Start from the open, flat DRESS and slide smoothly home to a loose, open schwa, with a good dose of 'AH' sprinkled on it!

Where the pears are scarce, the bears share theirs fairly.

TOUR: This set is beginning to be an endangered species by the 1980s, though it has by no means vanished completely. The original Sloane Rangers tended to still have the lovely slide from FOOT to their loose, open schwa, whereas by the 1990s they were more likely to use a THOUGHT or NURSE vowel.

> Muriel assured the poor tourists that the insurance was sure to cover Europe.

NB. See the note on page 145 regarding the PAW–POUR–POOR split!

Environmental Issues: ─────────────────

Vowel Clusters and Collisions:

Smoothing: Extreme

A general feature of all upper-class accents is the use of smoothing to a greater or lesser degree.

'Smoothing' refers to the 'smoothing out' of the vowel slides that happen when two or more vowels from the Kit List meet.

For example, in the word 'science', the PRICE vowel meets the schwa, making a slide through three shapes: 'A–I–UH'. To smooth this slide out, remove the middle shape completely, losing any feeling of 'Y' from the tongue, leaving you with 'SA–UNCE' or even 'SAHNCE'.

This also happens when words meet… Try saying the following, losing any feeling of 'W' or 'Y' between these words:

GO OUT   DO IT   PLAY ON

This accent uses *extreme* smoothing.

Hear It: Track 144.

fire ('fa-i-uh') smoothes to 'fah'

power ('pa-oo-uh') smoothes to 'pah'

throwing ('thruh-oo-ing') smoothes to 'thruhng'

Vowels followed by 'ER' and 'ING' are the most common to be subject to smoothing:

player   lawyer   mower   higher   tower

fleeing   drawing   doing   playing   bowing   lying   annoying

GOING: The very forward position of the tongue at the start of the GOAT vowel means that when it is said quickly, without any stress, there is not even a hint of a 'W' or lip-rounding in the middle of this word. 'Going home' = 'gung hum' or 'geng hem'.

Hear It: Track 145.

We were **going** to a party in **Lower** Loxeley, bowling along with considerable **power, trying** to get to it on time. 'Who are we **seeing** there?' I asked. 'Oh, some very **annoying** people', he answered. 'There'll be **Howard**, the incessant card **player**, and my Aunt the **lawyer, doing** her usual party piece. They'll be in the **drawing** room, gathered around the **fire, chewing** the fat, **playing** "who is the smartest", **allowing** no one else to get a word in. How **tire**some!'

Vowel Reductions: The little sounds with a big impact!

When a syllable has no weight, or stress in it, the vowel is 'reduced' to something shorter and less open than it would be otherwise. How many syllables are reduced, and which vowel is used can make a huge difference to the quality of the accent.

Older upper-class accents had a strong tendency to *minimise* the number of stressed syllables in a word, often stressing only one syllable in multisyllabic words. This meant that vowels were being reduced left, right and centre. The original Sloane Rangers weren't averse to this feature, as it maintained a clear class distinction. Here are some keywords that are stressed differently as a result:

Hear It: Track 146.

necessary = NEsusry   circumstances = CIRcumstunsiz
momentarily = MOmuntruly   finance = fuNANCE   portrait = PORtrut

This feature extends to *all* 'ORY', 'ARY', 'ONY', etc. endings.

inventory = INvuntry   library = LIbry   alimony = ALimuny

happY: This is a KIT vowel in most older upper-class accents. The Sloane Rangers kept the old-fashioned approach, using their version of a KIT shape that lurks in no-man's-land between KIT, DRESS and a commA vowel!

Hear It: Track 147.

Billy and Mary were happy to see the movie, 'When Harry Met Sally'. Billy had a coffee, and Mary bought a pastry.

FLEECE and **GOOSE** similarly the Sloane Rangers preferred to use their versions of the old-fashioned KIT and FOOT shapes in final unstressed positions, whereas the New Wave keep them as FLEECE and GOOSE.

He loves me   'We shall be   She was, was she?   Would you   The igloo

commA–lettER: Can be quite open and back. Almost a shortish 'AH'.

Hear It: *Track 148.*

gather   writer   anger   India   Diana   yoga

privATE word endings: By the 1980s these endings were beginning to change from the old-fashioned KIT vowel to a more modern, American-influenced schwa:

Hear It: *Track 149.*

toil**et** (bracelet, pamphlet, etc.) = TOI-l*ut*
priv**ate** (climate, etc.) = PRI-v*ut*
prob**lem** (system, Blenheim, etc.) = PROB-*lum*
kind**ness** (countless, business, etc.) = KIND-*nuss*

horsES word endings: And although the following little endings traditionally used a KIT vowel as they do in a NSEA, many of the Sloane Rangers began to use a commA vowel in these, again giving the words a 'cool', American quality.

hors**es** (foxes, daises, marries, etc.) = HOR-*suz*
wast**ed** (landed, excited, etc.) = WAS-*tud*
long**est** (biggest, forest, etc.) = LONG-*gust*
act**ive** (massive, etc.) = AC-*tuv*
pock**et** (biscuit, planet) = PO-*kut*
coll**ege** (sausage, baggage, package, etc.) = CO-*ludge*
sur**face** (office) = SUR-*fuss*

Finally, for our North American friends with good intentions we must mention and draw attention to the convention of...

TION endings: It is crucial that these have a tiny schwa, and not a nasalised KIT vowel in them. This tiny detail can be a real giveaway! For example:

Hear It: *Track 150.*

attention = *attenshun*, not *attenshin*
mission = *misshun*, not *misshin*
station = *stayshun*, not *stayshin*

A NOD TO THE NEW WAVE...

The class-based accents we have described so far take us up to the 1980s, and are therefore designed to help you with characters from the 20th century, but what of the 21st century? What has happened to class-based accents since then? What if your character is a young upper middle-class army officer, fashion student or musician, etc? In this final section we give you quick snapshots of three 'types' that you may find useful if you are playing contemporary upper and upper middle-class characters under the age of 40. They have all come hot on the heels of the accent innovators of the 1980s, the Sloane Rangers.

- **The Regular Set**, for the average Joes and Josephines, with no airs and graces, just comfy in their own skin.

- **The Chelsea Set**, for those younger adults still attached to the up-market style of West London, who are more than comfortable, or even proud of their class.

- **The Shoreditch Set**, for those young adults who are trying to blend in, who consciously or unconsciously hide their class, and who may have discovered the apparently cool alternative of London's East End scene.

> TOP TIP
>
> Before you read about each of these, you may want to check this overview of important features which identify a character as having been born after c.1975, and which all New Wave accents have in common, followed by a few extra sounds that will mark you out as having been to a top fee-paying school...

POST-1975 FEATURES

- **FOOT and GOOSE**: The shapes used in these two sets have changed radically since the days of the Imperial Lords and Ladies. No longer made by the back of the tongue, in the back of the mouth, with lovely low resonance, these have drifted forward over the years, so that the tongue shape in GOOSE, for example, can be very close to a KIT shape but with a little lip-rounding added on!

- **TRAP**: This set has a much more open shape. The old 'trep' days are gone.

- **Final 'Y'**: The days of the clipped KIT shape have gone. These are now long and sometimes extra long!

- **'WH'**: The 'W-WH' distinction died out long ago!

NEW WAVE

How To Do Standard English Accents

- **'YOOs'**: Even the use of the 'YOO' is waning. It has all but disappeared after an 'L' (allude) and an 'S' (suit) although still firmly present after 'T' (tune) and 'D' (duty) where it is likely to be crunched.

- **L Effect on GOAT–Goal**: This distinction is now the accepted form. Not to distinguish these shapes will definitely make your character sound old-fashioned!

- **Word Stress**: The preference for stressing as few syllables as possible is being eroded, possibly by the influence of West Coast American, as well as Northern English accents. Anyone saying the word 'circumstances' as 'SUHcumstunsiz' or 'necessary' as 'NEsusry' will sound very old hat, so put those syllables back in!

And add the following four vowels and some smoothing to the mix to mark yourself out as having been to a top fee-paying school…

GOOSE: Make a KIT shape with the tongue, then round the lips a little. Make the word GOOGLE rhyme with GIGGLE!!

FLEECE: Keep this very high and tight, squeezed onto the gum-ridge.

NURSE: As open as you can, and quite far back, get this to almost merge with BATH–PALM–START.

GOAT: Keep this TINY and very close to the gum-ridge at the front of the mouth. Again, get the tongue close to a KIT shape.

SMOOTHING: Don't say fire, say 'FAH', don't say 'HIGHER' say 'HAH', and you are not going or doing, you 'GENG' and 'DING'!

Now read on for our **Nod to the New Wave**…

THE REGULAR SET

Hear It: Tracks 151–153.

Listen first to the Kit List (*Track 151*) and then to either the male speaker (*Track 152*) or female speaker (*Track 153*).

These are lovely examples of contemporary, good-egg, middle of the road, upper middle-class speakers aged up to about 45. This sound is neither pushing, nor hiding its class. It is extremely relaxed. It can be heard in many walks of life, from the armed forces to the City (the financial district), from business to farming.

Regular Set: Prince William, Prince Edward, Dominic West, Sam West, Matthew Macfadyen, Anna Chancellor, Keira Knightley, Sienna Miller, Emily Blunt, Boris Johnson, Emma Watson.

The GROOVE

Tune: You can either use as little tune as possible, as with our two example speakers, or you could add some large final cadences, dropping the voice down and back, for an extra air of certainty.

Rhythm: Our male speaker avoids landing heavily on any words in order not to sound too authoritative, whereas our female speaker really lands on some of the key words in order to demonstrate her enthusiasm and sense of drama.

The FOUNDATIONS

- **Setting**: Keep the jaw a little bit slack and the face relaxed. The soft palate feels a little high. The tongue tip lifts and gently taps the gum-ridge.
- **Zone**: Aim for Zone 2, but hold some of the sound back into Zone 5.
- **Tone**: It has a warm tone, not unlike NSEA, but a little 'muffled' and lacking in brightness due to the lack of facial engagement and the use of Zone 5.
- **Direction**: Flows gently forwards.

The Bite

'T': 'Ts' between vowels will often be voiced as a 'D':

    bedder   lodda

NEW WAVE

The Shapes

Here are seven key shapes that distinguish this accent from a NSEA accent:

Hear It: Track 151. 'The Kit List'.

GOOSE: Push this right forward all the way into the KIT territory!

> Two beautiful youths moved through a few juicy rude grooves in feudal confusion.

FLEECE: Keep this high, tight and bright.

> The police had reason to believe that Peter, Keith and the anaemic Sheila were in league to illegally deceive people.

LOT–CLOTH: Keep it back in Zone 5 and round the lips.

> (merged) Tom and Ross had coffee and sausages on a top-notch yacht in Boston.

THOUGHT–NORTH–FORCE: Keep it back in Zone 5, round the lips.

> (merged) Paul applauded George as he cavorted with all the naughty daughters who yawned when Thor taught them of war with chalk and talk in York.

GOAT–GOAL: VERY forward! Start almost at DRESS and slide to KIT while rounding the lips. But the L Effect does come into play on GOAL words (bolder, controlling and soldier).

> Joan coaxed her beau, Owen, to grow bolder, though she loathed over-controlling soldiers.

MOUTH: Ends only in schwa, no rounding!

> The loud crowd from south of the county wanted to oust the clown out of town, but they were all mouth.

Smoothing:

Vowel clusters smooth quite noticeably! (see pages 145-146 for a full description.)

> Fire = Fah   Power = Pah   Going = Geng, etc...

THE CHELSEA SET

Hear It: *Tracks 154 – 157.*

Listen first to the Kit List (*Track 154*) and then either to the male speaker (*Track 155*) or one of the female speakers (*Tracks 156 and 157*).

These three speakers are examples of a contemporary breed of **Sloane Ranger**. The first two have a younger sound, whilst the third is a great example of the older **It Girl**. They would be equally useful as a models for young officers, City Boys and Girls (the financial whizz kids), fashionistas and yummy mummies. Younger speakers add a dose of 'cool' to their sound by using West Coast American influenced sounds. These are the more expensive, haute couture, socialites who are more than comfortable with their class.

Chelsea Set: Most of the people in *Made In Chelsea*, Tara Palmer-Tomkinson, Sarah Beeny, Tamara and Petra Ecclestone.

The GROOVE

Tune: The tune is very flat. Younger speakers (18-30) often use a lot of up-speak (rising inflections) throughout linking phrases. They may even use up-speak as final cadences before a full stop, especially the girl!

Rhythm: The rhythm is very uneven, with sudden bursts of pace that then settle into a slow stretched vowel. Girls often use stretches, pitch-glides and vocal creak on final vowels.

The FOUNDATIONS

- **Setting**: The soft palate is tense: whether high or low, it is taut! The It Girls are also likely to pinch the 'sniff' muscles either side of the nose, tensing the top lip and flaring the nostrils.
- **Zone**: 3-5. The voice is held back and can be quite pharyngeal (dropping into Zone 5) or quite nasal (driving into Zone 6/7).
- **Tone**: If the soft palate is high and tense it leads to a muffled tone, whereas the low, tense soft palate of the It Girls leads to sharp overtones.
- **Direction**: Tricky to pin down, younger speakers spin the sound around Zone 5, whereas our It Girl drives her sound into the hard palate and behind the nose.

NEW WAVE

The Bite

The speed of this variety can lead to the sorts of drops and crunches more often associated with regional accents, though this is not true of the older It Girl who maintains clearly articulated consonants.

- **'L'**: Traditionally dark 'Ls' (before a consonant and in final positions) may be dropped, but they are not replaced by a 'W'.
- **'ING'**: May be dropped, along with the 'T', in phrases like 'trying to' (tryn'a), 'going to' (gunn'a).
- **'T'**: Can have all the issues! It is very likely to be voiced as a 'D', replaced with a Glottal Stop, crunched, or dropped completely.

   Voiced as a 'D': better = bedda   get a = gedda

   Replaced by a soft Glottal Stop: better = be?uh   get a = ge?uh

   Crunched: tuesday = chewsday   would you = woodjoo

   Dropped: twenty = twenny

The Shapes

Here are seven key shapes that distinguish this accent from a NSEA:

Hear It: Track 154. 'The Kit List'.

KIT: Flatten a little towards a DRESS vowel or even a schwa.

   The ship listed as busy women built a pretty bridge in the dim mid-winter.

DRESS: Flatten towards the STRUT territory.

   In a sweat Jeff edged his head into the Thames in an effort to save his best friend from the treacherous bell of death.

STRUT: Sprinkle a little TRAP onto the sound.

   The dull young monks rushed to hunt the buds of the lovely buttercups.

GOOSE: Push this right forward and sprinkle it with a KIT quality (we once mistook the word Google for Giggle when listening to a Chelsea Set girl!)

   Two beautiful youths moved through a few juicy rude grooves in feudal confusion.

NURSE: Pull it back to almost merge with BATH–PALM–START. Use a big sprinkle of 'Ahhh'!

   Pearl urged Myrtle's attorney to rehearse a certain circus turn before the courteous worm turned.

TRAP: Sprinkle a good dose of BATH–PALM–START on this too!
The cat dashed to catch the ham that dangled from the bag.

GOAT–Goal: VERY forward. Start from a raised schwa and tighten towards KIT. The L Effect is likely to come into play on GOAL words (bolder, controlling and soldier), but this is not essential.
Joan coaxed her beau, Owen, to grow bolder, though she loathed over-controlling soldiers.

PRICE: Our It Girl starts from a nasalised BATH vowel and swiftly drives to a tight FLEECE.
Friday is the right night to arrive by bicycle in Cyprus to buy a fine eiderdown.

SQUARE: Very open and held in the yawn.
Where the pears are scarce, the bears share theirs fairly.

Vowel Reductions

These little endings have a KIT vowel in a NSEA, but like the Sloane Rangers you may hear the Chelsea Set using a schwa in these, giving the words a 'cool', American quality.

horses (foxes, daises, marries, etc.) = HOR-suz
wasted (landed, excited, etc.) = WAS-tud
longest (biggest, forest, etc.) = LONG-gust
active (massive, etc.) = AC-tuv
pocket (biscuit, planet) = PO-kut
college (sausage, baggage, package, etc.) = CO-ludge
surface (office) = SUR-fus

happY and FLEECE endings: These have a tighter FLEECE vowel, which girls especially may really hold and stretch at the ends of phrases.
I'm really happeeeee. I think he fancies meeeee. I'd love a coffeeeee.

Smoothing:

Vowel clusters smooth quite noticeably! (see pages 145-146 for a full description.)
Fire = Fah   Power = Pah   Going = Geng, etc…

NEW WAVE

THE SHOREDITCH SET

Hear It: Tracks 158–160

Listen first to the Kit List (*Track 158*) and then either to the female speaker (*Track 159*) or male speaker (*Track 160*).

Our next two examples are from the Shoreditch Set. Unlike the Chelsea Set these young people are usually trying to blend with a set of colleagues from a mixed social background, and as such they may be inclined to hide their class, consciously or unconsciously. They add a dose of 'cool' to their sound through East London influenced sounds. Some are the 'anti-fashion' fashionistas, dedicated to the retro, thrift-shop look. They like small, independent coffee bars, small, independent pubs, and small, independent bands! This accent can also be heard in the world of the armed forces and sports, and a variety of this accent can even be heard among young Royals!

Shoreditch Set: Ellie Kendrick, Zara Phillips, Prince Harry, Matt Smith, Olly Alexander.

The GROOVE

Tune: Again you will hear the VERY flat tune and quite a lot of up-speak as with the Chelsea Set.

Rhythm: The pace is VERY fast! Spread the weight evenly and thinly across the phrase without drawing attention to words in order to avoid any 'authoritative' or assertive qualities. The dropped consonants and Glottal Stops add a choppy quality to the rhythm.

The FOUNDATIONS

- **Setting**: There is very little engagement of the articulatory muscles…very cool!
- **Zone**: Sounds like it wants to come forward but is being held back behind Zone 2!
- **Direction**: Choppy and lurching forward, like a badly driven car!

The Bite

The speed of this variety leads to all sorts of drops and crunches more often associated with regional accents:

- **'R'**: The intrusive bounce so frowned upon by their parents may make a strong re-appearance! (Edda Rand Jan. Law Rand order.)
- **'L'**: Traditionally dark 'Ls' (before a consonant and in a final position) are dropped and may be replaced by a gentle 'W'.
- **'ING'**: These can be regularly dropped in speedy sections of speech.
- **'H'**: You may hear the occasional 'H' drop.
- **'TH'**: You may even hear 'F' replacement being used in some words!
- **'T'**: Can have all the issues! It is very likely to be voiced as a 'D', replaced with a Glottal Stop, crunched, or dropped completely.
  Voiced as a 'D': better = bedda   get a = gedda
  Replaced by a soft Glottal Stop: better = be?uh   get a = ge?uh
  Crunched: tuesday = chewsday   would you = woodjoo
  Dropped: twenty = twenny can have all the issues:
- **'TL'**: (lateral plosion, page 123) Can have Major Issues, with the 'T' in words such as 'little' being either dropped: 'li'l'; replaced by a Glottal Stop: 'li?le'; or replaced by a 'D': 'liddle', all with the final 'L' being replaced by a gentle 'W'!

The Shapes

Here are eight key shapes that distinguish this accent from NSEA:

Hear It: Track 158. 'The Kit List'.

KIT: Flatten a little towards the schwa.

The ship listed as busy women built a pretty bridge in the dim mid-winter.

DRESS: Flatten and sprinkle a huge dose of TRAP on it.

In a sweat Jeff edged his head into the Thames in an effort to save his best friend from the treacherous bell of death.

FOOT: Very forward, in the KIT territory (also see L Effect below).

The woman shouldn't put the full pudding onto the butcher's hook.

GOOSE: Push this right forward towards KIT (also see L Effect below).

Two beautiful youths moved through a few juicy rude grooves in feudal confusion.

NEW WAVE

GOAT–Goal: You can really hear a London quality in this shape. Start from a STRUT position and slide to the schwa, and use the full L Effect on GOAL words (bolder, controlling, soldier).

Joan coaxed her beau, Owen, to grow bolder, though she loathed over-controlling soldiers.

PRICE: You can really hear a London quality in this shape too! Start from a STRUT position and slide to a tight FLEECE position.

Friday is the right night to arrive by bicycle in Cyprus to buy a fine eiderdown.

MOUTH: Ends only in schwa, no rounding, again giving it a London quality.

The loud crowd from south of the county wanted to oust the clown out of town, but they were all mouth.

NEAR: This is a long steady vowel lurking between KIT and DRESS.

Maria was sincere in her weird career but feared the fierce bearded cashier.

See the note on page 145 regarding the PAW–POUR–POOR split!

Environmental Issues

L Effect: Shoreditchers are particularly keen on the London-style L Effect, often replacing final 'Ls' with a 'W'. Because of this FOOT, GOOSE and GOAT shapes get pulled back out of their forward position towards the 'OO' of the replacement 'W'.

foot–full   goose–ghoul   goat–goal

happY and FLEECE endings: these have a tighter FLEECE vowel which girls especially may really hold and stretch at the ends of phrases.

I'm really happeeeee. I think he fancies meeeee. I'd love a coffeeeee.

Smoothing

The smoothing of vowel clusters associated with other upper and upper-middle-class accents is not used in this accent. Instead vowel clusters may glide as in a NSEA or even bounce as in London accents.

Fire = fi–yuh.   Power = pa–wuh.   Going = gu–wing.

7

GET PROFESSIONAL

7

IN THIS CHAPTER...

Assuming you aren't simply doing accents as a hobby, you will also need to know how to take your work in the professional arena to a professional level. This means knowing not just how to **do** a Standard English Accent, but also how to **work on** it to keep improving it and how to **work with** it in different professional contexts.

First of all we will give you advice on how to **get practising**: after all, if you want to be professional at something you have to practise.

We then take you through what to do when your accent meets the specific demands of:

- the production
- the director
- the rehearsal
- the character

And finally:

- How to handle an audition
- How to handle sight-reading

GET PRACTISING

It ought to go without saying (but it often doesn't) that if you want to be good at something it takes practice. This doesn't mean having to sit for hours labouring over your script: it simply means building a little bit of accent practice into your daily routine.

It is absolutely essential to practise both on and off your text. If the only things you can say in the accent are the words in your script, you do not know the accent and your performance will be limited. What happens when someone forgets their cue and you have to ad lib? Or there's a re-write, or a cut reappears? You're scuppered!

The basic practice material is the Kit List, the Practice Sentences and *Arthur the Rat* (see page 225).

Here's some more advice for accent practice.

Springboard sentence

● Have a 'springboard sentence' in the accent. This is a short phrase that automatically gets the accent into your mouth, seemingly without you being involved. Your brain associates that phrase with the accent and as soon as you say it that 'accent file' in your head downloads and opens up. This is invaluable for those moments when you seem to go adrift and need to 'reboot' the accent.

Out in the real world

● Read billboards, adverts, notices and other short bursts of text either out loud or in your head. This trains you to translate from the written word into the new spoken patterns of an accent.

● Look out for specific sounds and see if you can identify them on billboards, etc.

● Ask for directions, or for assistance in a shop, using the accent.

Anytime, anywhere

● Listen to your accent resource (the Kit List, the Practice Sentences, *Arthur the Rat* or some free speech) a little every day. You can do this while you're getting a meal ready, in the car, at the gym, even as you go to sleep; anywhere that makes it easy and regular. It is vital to give your brain something to refer to and feed off.

7

- Narrate your day: 'I think I'll just put the kettle on', 'Oh, that's the phone, I'll just answer it', and so on. Notice and correct any mistakes as you make them. It's crucial not to reinforce bad habits but to teach yourself the new patterns. Horsey types will tell you that if you let a horse refuse a jump once the chances are it will refuse it again, and we can tell you that your mouth behaves in much the same way. Remember, just like the rider, you are the one in charge, not your mouth, so make sure you *always* correct it at every jump!

- If there's a group of you learning the accent, have an accent evening: you could cook food, listen to the music, watch the movies, whatever takes your fancy. Any excuse for a party!

- Don't just practise the bits you're good at. Focus on different elements of the accent – the Foundations, the Bite, the Vowel Shapes or the Groove.

With the Set Text

- Practise with the Set Text (*Arthur the Rat*) and Kit List. The Set Text contains all the tricky sounds and combinations of the sounds in English, so once you can say this you can pretty well say everything!

- Record yourself. Play it back and be your own judge. If you don't convince yourself you won't convince anyone else either!

- The more you work with the Set Text and the Kit List, the more you will get to know them. Once you can confidently recite them in the accent they will be invaluable as warm-up and practice material.

On the script

Eventually, of course, your words will be connected to emotional impulses and actions, but there is also a certain amount of basic technical **gymnastics** that your mouth is going to have to get used to before you get there. This may be more or less challenging depending on the accent you are doing and your familiarity with it. Sometimes you need to let yourself off the 'emotional' hook and work on your script technically. This is only the same as doing table work and blocking in rehearsals. You do it with the acting, so do it with the accent.

- To begin with you may want to read very slowly out loud in your new accent, a little like a child learning to read, plotting your way through the sounds.

How To Do Standard English Accents

● Work on your text phrase by phrase.

● Identify words in the phrase that can take the stress. These will provide anchor sounds in the phrase. These stresses are only temporary, as things may change during rehearsals, but you need them as a starting point. Practise these words first so that you are confident in making the shapes and sounds. They will provide solid stepping stones through the text.

Practising your text is very much like practising a **gymnastics tumbling routine**. To begin with, you have to practise each of the moves separately before you can string them together. Once you are confident you stand at one corner of the floor mat, looking at the 'phrase' to be performed between there and the far corner. You breathe and... GO, landing with aplomb at the far corner. If anything does go wrong you know that bit needs reworking until the whole sequence is flawless. These are the steps:

1 Identify the 'big moves' in the routine – the triple sukahara, the double back flip and the handspring! These may be words you find tricky, or specific vowels or consonant combinations.

2 Work on each of these moves separately until your mouth can do them smoothly.

3 Practise getting both to and from each of these moves until you can get through the whole phrase fluently. If you falter, stumble or trip, keep going back to step two until you can say the whole phrase without tripping.

4 Once you are confident with the technical aspect of the gymnastics the next step for a perfect ten is to do it 'once more with feeling'. If when you connect to the emotional drive of the line things begin to slip, go back and look at those bits again. Connect the sound firmly to the feeling so that the two things become one.

> TOP TIP
> You only really know your lines when you can say them...
> ● technically
> ● fluently
> ● emotionally

7

ACCENT MEETS PRODUCTION

Over the years we have worked with many different kinds of actor and director, each with their own working process. Whatever that process may be, during any rehearsal period it is the actor's job to layer the journey of their character into the world of the play and the particular demands of the production.

Working with an accent adds another layer that will need to be woven into this process. It can be quite a delicate juggling act and one that will need careful consideration. On the one hand you don't want the accent to get in the way of your ability to focus, but on the other hand you want to be sure the accent is an integral part of the character. And of course, by the time you are in front of an audience you want the accent to be bedded in and authentic.

There is a lot to consider, and each of us finds our own way through, so here are some handy hints for getting the most out of yourself and your accent.

ACCENT MEETS DIRECTOR

You may work with some very different directorial approaches. We have known directors who:

● **Want you to speak all the time in the accent when in the rehearsal room.**
This can be heaven or hell. Experience tells us that at its worst this approach will ingrain bad habits which become fixed and difficult to correct. At best, however, it can be an opportunity to make an accent feel as natural as your own speech. If this is what your director wants, you will need to be *very* disciplined. Whenever you are using the accent you are effectively working on it. It is tough to have to concentrate this hard on the accent all day, every day.

● **Don't want you to use the accent for the first week.**
This is a very popular approach with directors. Be sure that you use your home time well to work on the accent and the text, as once they do ask you to use it they will expect the accent to be great! (See *Get Practising*, page 213.)

● **Wish they didn't have to deal with the accent at all!**
This is the director that doesn't want to know about the accent, has had bad experiences with dialect coaches, or has seen good actors go bad simply because of the accent! Well, that's a tricky one: you will have to

work independently and not expect any support. Try not to be dispirited by this and don't take it personally.

- **Want to give you accent notes.**
  Be grateful for the interest but know that they may not be the most sensitive or helpful remarks! If you are lucky enough to have a coach working on the show make sure you explain what your director has asked for so that together you can solve whatever problems arise.

Every director is unique, as is every actor, so whatever is happening make sure you are taking responsibility for yourself and your accent work. Look at *Get Practising* (page 213) to find suggestions for structured ways of working. The one thing we can say for certain is that you *cannot* start work on the accent too soon!

ACCENT MEETS REHEARSAL

Always warm up your accent before rehearsals begin. It can take a good ten minutes of talking in an accent before you are fully engaged with it.

Of course, in rehearsal you are two people, yourself and the character (You and the New):

- When you are yourself, talking as yourself, it helps to have a 'springboard sentence' to get back into the accent when the scene starts again (see *Springboard sentence*, page 213).

- When you are in character, but not actually speaking, maybe you are pausing, thinking, relaxing, or listening in a scene, **don't relax out of the muscular setting** of the accent! Remember, the setting of the accent *is* the relaxed setting of your character's face. Likewise, if you 'uhm' and 'erm' the sound you hear should be the hesitation sound of the accent, not your own.

If you have time between scenes when you are not called, you can use it to listen to your resource recording and practise your accent on or off script. If your accent is getting in the way of your work in a scene it is a clear sign that you need to do more work outside rehearsals. During the rehearsal of a scene is *not* the time to do this kind of work.

7

ACCENT MEETS CHARACTER

Age, gender, class, profession, family background and personal aspirations will all make a difference to the way someone sounds. Whatever acting process you have, connect your accent study to your character study.

Some actors use the following exercise to develop a character history/profile and it can also be a great way of getting to know the manner in which your character communicates.

● What do I say about other people?

● What do others say about me?

When you have answered those questions by looking through your script, find qualities within the accent that will help you portray them. You may think of the accent you are using as 'friendly', 'warm' and 'cuddly' but your character is referred to by others as 'spiteful', 'short-tempered' and 'cold'. Try to figure out what qualities within the accent can help you to portray these qualities. It may be in the Groove or the consonant quality or simply the pace of delivery.

If you can find a buddy, 'hot-seat' each other in the accent. This helps you to develop spontaneity and inner connection.

ACCENT MEETS AUDITION

You may have two weeks to prepare for an audition or you may have two days. You may be asked for a speech, or you may be asked to sight-read.

Ask yourself this question: **'How good am I at this accent?'** (Be honest with yourself.) Only then you can assess how much work you have to do and how much time you have to do it in.

There is always time to do something useful, even if you only have a day:

- Decide on the variety of Standard English Accent required for the character.

- If you want to go for a specific variety focus on the Foundations and Groove first. Remember, getting into the Groove can really help access the energy and drive of the character!

- If you know you have some 'issues' doing your Standard English Accent such as splashy 'Ts', trouble with dark 'Ls', a vowel you find difficult etc., go through the script to identify any tricky words and practise them.

- Have a springboard sentence ready to get you into the accent.

- If you don't have much time, or don't feel confident in a particular variety, you could simply do Traditional RP or even a NSEA, with the addition of the Foundations and/or the Groove of a particular variety.

The more time you have, the more detail you can go into.

On the day

Before you go into the casting/audition make sure you have warmed the accent up, that you've got your springboard sentence and that the accent is ready to be switched on. It is a tall order to expect to be able to pull it out of the bag the moment you open your mouth.

If it is a sight-reading audition (aagghhh!), the assumption is that you can do the accent. You must have said you can or you wouldn't be there in the first place! The chances are they will give you the text to look at just before you go in. Make sure you get what you do know of the accent into your system: read the script out loud; get it into your mouth and body; feel the muscularity, the zone and the energy and direction of flow. Remember: the purpose of sight-reading is to demonstrate your talents as an *actor* and your suitability for the role. Focus on your acting and script skills. The odd mistakes in an accent will be forgiven if you have shown willing and are acting with integrity.

Don't forget to act!

Even a polished accent can have its downside. Actors can get carried away by the sound of the accent and forget some of the most basic acting prerequisites such as: listen and respond; be in the moment; connect to the impulse; remember what you want; etc.

If they give you the script in advance, here are some basic **script skills** that don't take long and are invaluable to keep you connected to the drive of the text:

● Notice sentence lengths, punctuation, odd word use, etc.

● Mark the important/significant words.

● Mark the word at the end of each phrase and head towards it. The last word is so much more important than the first in terms of connection.

● Mark crescendos and changes of gear. Know the journey that your feelings and thoughts will move in.

While reading:

● Slow down your breathing. The most common mistake is to go too fast!

● Don't worry *at all* about being perfect. Be as good as you are. No better, no worse.

Finally, remember, they are interested in you as an *actor*, and will be more interested in an intelligent, professional approach to the accent and the acting. They want an actor with potential in the role, not just a polished mimic.

8

USEFUL STUFF

IN THIS CHAPTER

As we said in Get Professional, being good at an accent takes practice. In this chapter we have included the following practice material to help you get the basics right:

- The Kit List (page 223)
- Practice Sentences (page 223)
- *Arthur the Rat* (page 225)

On our website, www.howtodoaccents. com, you will also find marked up copies of *Arthur the Rat*, written phrase by phrase, to help you practise some of the Major Issues in Consonant Clusters:

- Dropped 'Hs'
- Crunches
- Nasal and Lateral Plosions
- Glottal Stops
- 'YOOs'

Having a basic understanding of your vocal equipment can really help. For this reason we have included:

- Knowing Your Equipment (page 226)

And for further reading please refer to our:

- Bibliography (page 232)
- Recommended Reading (page 232)

Finally, there is the essential list of MP3 tracks that accompany this book!

- MP3 Track List

For more Useful Stuff including practice speeches, videos, articles, and information on forthcoming workshops and publications go to www.howtodoaccents.com

NB. The all-important You and the New Chart filled in for a NSEA can also be found at www.howtodoaccents.com. Why not print this off and fill in your own accent details in the YOU section? An adapted and expanded version of Professor Wells' sets can be found on the *How to Do Accents* website, at **www.howtodoaccents.com**.

THE KIT LIST

For those of you who work with the International Phonetic Alphabet we have included the closest symbol to represent this sound.

KIT	ɪ	BATH	ɑː	FACE	eɪ
DRESS	e	PALM	ɑː	GOAT	əʊ
STRUT	ʌ	START	ɑː	PRICE	aɪ
FOOT	ʊ	LOT	ɒ	CHOICE	ɔɪ
GOOSE	uː	CLOTH	ɒ	MOUTH	aʊ
FLEECE	iː	THOUGHT	ɔː	NEAR	ɪə
NURSE	ɜː	NORTH	ɔː	SQUARE	eˑ (eə)
TRAP	a	FORCE	ɔː	TOUR	ɔː

PRACTICE SENTENCES

● **KIT** The ship listed as busy women built a pretty bridge in the dim mid-winter.

● **DRESS** In a sweat, Jeff edged his head into the Thames in an effort to save his best friend from the treacherous bell of death.

● **STRUT** The dull young monks rushed in a flood to hunt the buds of the lovely buttercup.

● **FOOT** The woman shouldn't put the full pudding onto the butcher's hook.

● **GOOSE** Two beautiful youths moved through a few smooth, juicy, rude grooves in feudal confusion.

● **FLEECE** The police had reason to believe that Peter, Keith and the anaemic Sheila could be in league to illegally deceive people.

● **NURSE** Pearl urged Myrtle's attorney to rehearse a certain circus turn before the courteous worm turned.

● **TRAP** The cat dashed to catch the ham that dangled from the bag.

● **BATH** 'Francis the calf can't dance', laughed Sandra the giraffe, aghast, as the calf pranced disastrously.

● **PALM** Brahms' sonata kept father calm in the spa.

● **START** Sergeant Charles was the star of the party with his hearty aria.

8

- **LOT** Tom honestly acknowledged how top-notch the swan was to dodge the yacht.

- **CLOTH** Ross often frothed the coffee and washed the long sausages in Boston.

- **THOUGHT** Paul applauded all the naughty daughters who yawned when taught with chalk and talk.

- **NORTH** George cavorted with Thor to fortify his short torso for the war in York.

- **FORCE** 'Of course I adore Nora', roared the porter through the door to the four divorced boarders.

- **FACE** April felt faint as she campaigned to rein in the wasteful ladies to change their ways and obey.

- **GOAT** Joan coaxed her beau, Owen, to grow bolder, though she loathed over-controlling soldiers.

- **PRICE** Friday is the right night to arrive by bicycle in Cyprus to buy a fine eiderdown.

- **CHOICE** The boy employed a joist to hoist the moist oysters into the boiling oil.

- **MOUTH** The loud crowd from south of the county wanted to oust the clown out of town, but they were all mouth.

- **NEAR** Maria was sincere in her weird career, but feared the fierce bearded cashier.

- **SQUARE** Where the pears are scarce, the bears share theirs fairly.

- **TOUR** Muriel assured the poor tourists that the insurance was sure to cover Europe.

SET TEXT: ARTHUR THE RAT

There was once a young rat named Arthur, who could never take the trouble to make up his mind. Whenever his friends asked him if he would like to go out with them, he would only answer, 'I don't know.' He wouldn't say 'yes' and he wouldn't say 'no' either. He could never learn to make a choice.

His aunt Helen said to him, 'No one will ever care for you if you carry on like this. You have no more mind than a blade of grass.' Arthur looked wise, but stupidly said nothing.

One rainy day, the rats heard a great noise in the loft where they lived. The pine rafters were all rotten in the middle, and at last one of the joists had given way and fallen to the ground. The walls shook and all the rats' hair stood on end with fear and horror. 'This won't do,' said the old rat who was chief, 'I'll send out scouts to search for a new home.'

Three hours later the seven tired scouts came back and said, 'We have found a stone house, which is just what we wanted; there is room and good food for us all. There is a kindly horse named Nelly, a cow, a calf, and a garden with flowers and an elm tree.' Just then the old rat caught sight of young Arthur. 'Are you coming with us?' he asked. 'I don't know,' Arthur sighed. 'The roof may not come down just yet.' 'Well,' said the old rat angrily, 'we can't wait all day for you to make up your mind. Right about face! March!' And they went straight off.

Arthur stood and watched the other little rats hurry away. The idea of an immediate decision was too much for him. 'I'm going back to my hole for a bit,' he said to himself dreamily, 'just to make up my mind.' That Tuesday night there was a great crash that shook the earth and down came the whole roof. Next day some men rode up and looked at the ruins. One of them moved a board and hidden under it they saw a young rat lying on his side, quite dead, half in and half out of his hole.

8

KNOWING YOUR EQUIPMENT

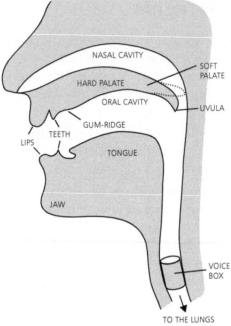

The articulators divide into two groups:

Passive (non-moving)

1   Teeth

2   Upper gum-ridge

3   Hard palate

Active (moving)

1   Lips/cheeks

2   (Lower) Jaw

3   Tongue

4   Soft palate

You will need a mirror so you can see what we are talking about!

The non-movable or **passive articulators** are the ones you're just stuck with (unless you have surgery…). Using your tongue, explore the *passive* articulators and connect what you feel to the diagram.

It is the passive articulators that provide the structures against which the **active articulators** play. The *active* articulators are the ones that do all the work.

Using the mirror, explore your *active* articulators:

1 LIPS and CHEEKS:

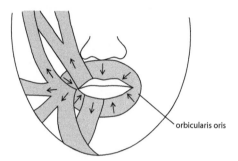

orbicularis oris

The muscles of the lips and cheeks are interconnected.

Your **lips** have one principal muscle called the *orbicularis oris*. This muscle divides into *inner* and *outer sphincter* actions. When you use the outer sphincter your lips can round like this:

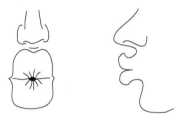

and when you use the inner sphincter they round like this:

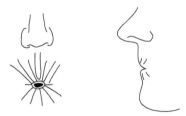

Some accents prefer one of these actions above another. Some like to make a proper circle, using a lot of rounding, while some use almost no rounding at all. Your **cheeks** have three principal muscle groups which pull the mouth in various directions:

- **sideways** into smiles, grins, etc.
- **downwards** into a grimace
- **upwards** into sneers

8

Try making these faces to see and feel these muscles at work. One or other of these muscles may be habitually loose or tight, active or passive in an accent.

2 JAW:

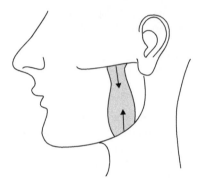

The lower jaw is attached to the upper jaw by muscle and ligament. To find this muscle, clench your teeth as if you are biting something with your back teeth. As you do this, put your fingers on your cheeks, just in front of your ears. You will feel the jaw muscle (the masseter) bunching. Try to picture how much space you have between your top and bottom teeth at the back as you sit at rest. The larger the space (without pulling), the looser the muscle. The jaw muscle holds different degrees of tension and looseness in different individuals and different accents.

3 TONGUE:

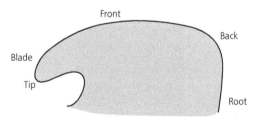

Front

Back

Blade

Tip

Root

The tongue is a surprisingly large organ. It is probably bigger than you think. It often surprises people that the entire body of muscle, right down to the underside of the chin, is in fact your tongue. Feel under your chin with your thumb while you push your tongue up against the roof of your mouth. What you feel pushing down against your thumb is your tongue! Look at your tongue in the mirror. It's a bit like a separate creature living in your mouth. In fact, it is probably the most flexible and sensitive muscle in the human body. Look in the mirror to see the different sections of your tongue. To begin with, notice that your tongue divides into two main sections: a 'free' section and an 'attached' section. Look under the tongue and you will see the bit where it attaches to the jaw. This free section is the most flexible bit and is sub-divided into the **Tip** and the **Blade**. This tends to be the bit of the tongue we are most aware of. The attached section is the bit you probably overlook. This part of the tongue is sub-divided into the **Front**, **Centre**, **Back** and **Root**. The tongue will have areas of tension and looseness developed through the habitual movements of the language and accent it makes.

4 SOFT PALATE:

If the front of your tongue is super-flexible, you can feel your way back along the roof of your mouth, curling your tongue back on itself until you feel a ridge. That is the end of the hard palate and the beginning of the soft palate. Get a mirror, and look at the little punch bag that dangles in the back of your mouth (you'll need to get the light in the right place to see inside). That's your **Uvula**. It hangs from the very end of the soft palate. (You can stun someone at a party with that piece of information!) The job of the soft palate is to direct the breath or voice into either the nose or the mouth. In some accents, such as Manchester and Essex, the soft palate is held low, giving the sound a lot of 'nasal spill'; in some, such as West Ireland and North Yorkshire it is high, creating a more oral sound; while in others, such as a NSEA, it has to bounce gymnastically up and down. Look again at the picture on page 226 and you will see how it can open or close the

8

passage to the nose. So you can see that having a flexible soft palate is essential in order to do accents.

● To see the soft palate *lift up* and close the passageway to your *nose*, make a yawn while keeping your tongue flat and forward in your mouth. You'll see the little punch bag shoot up and disappear. Make an 'AH' as you do this and feel the sound resonating in the mouth.

● To see it *drop down* and close the passageway to your *mouth*, open your mouth and say 'NG', the sound from the end of the word **sing**. You will see the back of the tongue and the soft palate come together and feel the sound resonating in the nose.

● To feel it *bounce* switch from the closed 'NG' to the yawned 'AH' in one action. If your soft palate is a bit sluggish, the 'AH' will end up in your nose! See if you can switch the direction of sound from your nose to your mouth. You may need to give it a bit of exercise to tone up that muscle!

So those are your **articulators**. But of course, they only form speech when they have something to play with, and that's where your voice box comes in…

5 VOICE BOX:

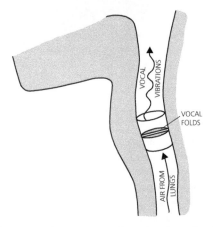

As the air leaves your lungs it passes through a piece of equipment called your **voice box** (also called the **larynx**). This 'box' contains two folds of flesh (**vocal folds**) that can either stay open to let air pass through unimpeded, or come together so that the outgoing air produces vibrations as it moves through them. You can see the voice box in the front of your neck. It's what a lot of us call the 'Adam's Apple'. Put your fingers on your neck and swallow and you will feel it bounce up and down. Men's voice boxes are generally larger than women's and consequently they make lower notes.

To feel your voice vibrations 'switching on and off' try the following:

● Make a long 'V' and, without stopping the air flow, change it to an 'F'. You will feel the voice switch off.

● Reverse this: start with an 'F' and change it to a 'V'. You will feel the voice switch on.

● On one breath change from 'F' to 'V' a number of times. You will feel the voice switching on and off as the folds come together then apart, together, then apart.

You can do the same thing with an 'S' and 'Z' too. If you feel your face, neck and chest as you make voice vibrations you can feel the vibrations resonating. Speech sounds are made with both breath and voice vibrations. (You will often see this distinction described as 'voiced' and 'voiceless'; see pages 114-117.) Your articulators play with the air and vibrations in your mouth, holding them, diverting them, and shaping them to create the specific speech sounds of your language and accent.

So that's your bits!

Of course, the really clever thing is the way we move them about and bring them together. Make an 'FF' sound and you'll feel your top teeth contact your bottom lip. Add voice vibrations to this shape and the sound changes to a 'V'. Make a 'K' and you're feeling the back of the tongue lift up to contact the soft palate. Add voice vibrations and you're making a 'G'.

With all these moving parts, awareness and flexibility are the key. If you want to improve your basic voice use then it may help to invest in a good voice book such as *Finding Your Voice* by Barbara Houseman, or *The Voice Book* by Michael McCallion. (See *Bibliography* and *Other Recommended Reading*, page 232.)

8

BIBLIOGRAPHY

Gwyneth L. Thurburn, *Voice and Speech* (James Nisbet and Co Ltd., 1939)

Clifford Turner, *Voice and Speech in the Theatre* (A & C Black, 1950)

J.C. Wells, *Accents of English: An Introduction* (CUP, 1982)

J.C. Wells, *Accents of English: The British Isles* (CUP, 1982)

J.C. Wells, *English Intonation, An Introduction* (CUP, 2006)

O'Connor and Arnold, *Intonation of Colloquial English* (Longman, 1973)

McCrum, Cran and MacNeil, *The Story of English* (Faber and Faber, 1987)

Beverley Collins and Inger Mees, *Practical Phonetics and Phonology* (Routledge, 2003)

OTHER RECOMMENDED READING

Voice Books

Cicely Berry, *Voice and the Actor* (John Wiley and Sons, 1991)

Barbara Houseman, *Finding Your Voice* (Nick Hern Books, 2002)

Malcolm Morrison, *Clear Speech* (A & C Black, 2001)

Michael McCallion, *The Voice Book* (Faber & Faber, 1998)

Christina Gutekunst and John Gillett, *Voice into Acting* (Bloomsbury, 2014)

Accent Books

Melvyn Bragg, *The Adventure of English* (Sceptre, 2003)

Melvyn Bragg & Simon Elms, *The Routes of English, Vol. 2* (BBC, 2000)

Cambridge English Pronouncing Dictionary (Cambridge, 2011)

Longman Pronunciation Dictionary (Longman, 2000)

FULL MP3 TRACK LISTING

PART 1
01 NSEA Arthur the Rat
02 NSEA Free Speech

NSEA Foundations
03 NSEA Zone 2
04 SEA Zone 1-7
05 3 Tones
06 Hesitation Sounds
08 NSEA Hesitation Sound

NSEA Groove
09 Groove only; Arthur the Rat
10 Dab & Glide; Arthur the Rat
11 Laban Action; Arthur the Rat
12 Default Tunes; Liverpool & NSEA
13 Intonation
14 3 Falls & 3 Rises
15 Building a Phrase
16 4 Sentence Types
17 10 Combinations

NSEA Planet Non Rhotic
18 R Drop
19 Mid Word Bounce
20 Linking R

NSEA Shapes
21 NSEA KIT List
22 Whispered Vowels
23 NSEA KIT
24 NSEA DRESS
25 NSEA STRUT
26 NSEA FOOT
27 NSEA GOOSE
28 NSEA FLEECE
29 NSEA NURSE
30 NSEA TRAP
31 NSEA BATH-PALM-START
32 NSEA LOT-CLOTH
33 NSEA THOUGHT-NORTH-FORCE-TOUR
34 NSEA FACE
35 NSEA GOAT
36 NSEA PRICE
37 NSEA CHOICE
38 NSEA MOUTH
39 NSEA NEAR
40 NSEA SQUARE
41 Gliding Cluster

42 Vowel Clusters
43 + ER + ING
44 NSEA Lower Loxeley
45 Bit v Bin Pairs
46 Bit/Bin Paragraph
47 Cat v Carry
48 Cat/Carry Paragraph
49 L Effect
50 L Effect Pairs
51 L Effect Paragraph
52 L Effect Flux
53 commA—lettER 1
54 commA—lettER 2
55 Y Endings
56 Y Endings Paragraph
57 privATE/ horsES
58 Cons/Coms/Obs
59 of what was because

NSEA Bite Major Players
60 R Sentence
61 R Words
62 L Sentence
63 NSEA Light L
64 NSEA Dark L
65 H Sentence
66 NG Sentence
67 TH Sentence
68 TH-TH+

NSEA Major Issues
69 Voiced and Voiceless Pairs
70 De-voicing
71 Voicing
72 Splashy T, Clean T
73 Dropped T
74 Crunch and Un-crunch
75 NO over-egging
76 TN & DN Words
77 TL & DL Words
78 NSEA YOOs
79 Traditional RP YOOs
80 Crunched YOOs

PART 2

Traditional RP
81 Traditional RP
82 TRP Foundations
83 TRP Linking R
84 TRP NO Intrusive R

85 TRP R T WH YOO
86 TRP KIT and List Sentences
87 TRP Smoothing
88 TRP Lower Loxeley
89 TRP Syllable Drops
90 TRP Short Endings
91 commA—lettER
92 privATE/horsES
93 TION Endings

Imperial Lords and Ladies
94 Imperial L&L Arthur
95 Imp L&L Foundations
96 Imp L&L Linking R
97 Imp L&L Intrusive R
98 Imp L&L Major Players
99 Imp L&L Major Issues
100 Imp L&L KIT list
101 Imp L&L Smoothing
102 Imp L&L Lower Loxeley

Military, Matrons & The Landed Gentry
103 MM&LG Arthur The Rat
104 MM&LG Foundations
105 MM&LG Linking R
106 MM&LG Major players & Issues
107 MM&LG KIT list
108 MM&LG Smoothing
109 MM&LG Lower Loxeley
110 MM&LG Syllable Drops
111 MM&LG Short Endings
112 MM&LG commA—lettER
113 MM&LG privATE/horsES
114 MM&LG TION

Debs, Dandies & Bright Young Things
115 DD&BYT Arthur the Rat
116 DD&BYT Foundations
117 DD&BYT Link/Intrusive R
118 DD&BYT Major Players/Issues
119 DD&BYT KIT list
120 DD&BYT Smoothing
121 DD&BYT Lower Loxeley
122 DD&BYT Syllable drops
123 DD& BYT Short Endings
124 DD&BYT commA—lettER

125 DD&BYT privATE/horsES
126 DD&BYT TION

Wartime Wendies & BBC Berties
127 WW&BB Arthur the Rat
128 WW&BB Foundations
129 WW&BB Linking R
130 WW&BB Major Players/ Issues
131 WW&BB KIT list
132 WW&BB Smoothing
133 WW&BB Lower Loxeley
134 WW&BB Syllable drops
135 WW&BB Short Endings
136 WW&BB commA—lettER
137 W&BB privATE/horsES
138 WW&BB TION

Sloane Rangers
139 Sloane Arthur the Rat
140 Sloane Foundations
141 Sloane Linking/Intrusive R
142 Sloane Major Players/Issues
143 Sloane Ranger KIT list
144 Sloane Smoothing
145 Sloane Lower Loxeley
146 Sloane Syllable Drops
147 Sloane Short Ending
148 Sloane commA—lettER
149 Sloane privATE/horsES
150 Sloane TION

Regular Set
151 Regular set KIT list
152 Regular set; Male
153 Regular set; Female

Chelsea Set
154 Chelsea set Kit List
155 Chelsea set; Male
156 Chelsea set; Female 1
157 Chelsea set; Female 2

Shoreditch Set
158 Shoreditch set Kit List
159 Shoreditch set; Male
160 Shoreditch set; Female

Old Wave
161 The Old Wave

8

TO DOWNLOAD THE MP3 RESOURCE PACK

To download the MP3 resource pack:

Open your internet browser and go to **https://www.bloomsbury.com/uk/ how-to-do-standard-english-accents-download-your-audio-files/**

1. Click the download link in the middle of the page

2. A compressed zip file (StandardEnglishAccents.zip) will automatically begin downloading

3. Once it has finished, go to the designated download folder on your computer

4. Right click on StandardEnglishAccents.zip, and click 'Extract'

5. When prompted enter the password: **HTDSEA521**

6. This will open a folder named Standard English Accents Resource Pack, containing 161 audio MP3 files

7. Simply drag and drop or copy and paste these files to wherever you wish to store them on your computer

If you require any further technical support, please contact **info@oberonbooks.com**

NOTES

8

8

8

www.howtodoaccents.com